The 1919 World Series

The 1919 World Series

What Really Happened?

WILLIAM A. COOK

McFarland & Company, Inc., Publishers
Jefferson, North Carolina, and London

Library of Congress Cataloguing-in-Publication Data

Cook, William A., 1944–
        The 1919 World Series: what really happened? / William A. Cook
        p.   cm.
        Includes bibliographical references and index.
        ISBN 0-7864-1069-8 (softcover : 50# alkaline paper) ∞
        1. World Series (Baseball) (1919).   2. Baseball — United States —
    History — 20th century. I. Title.
        GV878.4.C66   2001
        796.357'646 — dc21   2001030377

British Library Cataloguing data are available

Manufactured in the United States of America

*McFarland & Company, Inc., Publishers
    Box 611, Jefferson, North Carolina 28640
        www.mcfarlandpub.com*

Contents

Introduction

During my lifetime, which is all too rapidly approaching six decades, it seems like I have read five hundred or more various newspaper articles, magazine stories and other journalistic blurbs about the 1919 World Series between the Cincinnati Reds and Chicago White Sox. Incredible as it may be, every one of these ramblings has a common theme. They all end up stating one way or another that if eight Chicago players had not collaborated with gamblers to fix the 1919 World Series, the White Sox would have just clobbered the hapless National League Champion Cincinnati Reds.

I grew up in Cincinnati as a Reds fan and later lived in Chicago, thereby evolving into a White Sox fan. Consequently, I had the opportunity to see games played in both Crosley Field (Redland Field) and Comiskey Park and have heard the fable of the 1919 World Series told in various versions, depending of course on where the story is being told. During my Cincinnati experience when I was a patron at the now defunct Shipley's Bar & Grill in Clifton Heights, I heard the Reds version of the 1919 World Series. Likewise, during my Chicago experience when I was a patron at the now defunct Stock Yards Inn in Bridgeport, I heard the White Sox version of the 1919 World Series.

Now, it is certainly not uncommon for reasonable people to examine historical events and reach different conclusions on the outcomes. Therefore, as a reasonable person, and after researching and analyzing the events

1

that took place during the controversial 1919 World Series, I have reached the conclusion, contrary to popular belief, that it makes little difference if the series was tainted with a conspiracy of eight White Sox players to throw games or not. The Cincinnati Reds won the 1919 World Series and would have won any way it was played — fair, fixed, tainted or otherwise.

Among the more recent and popular events that have perpetuated a lot of misinformation regarding to the 1919 World Series is the 1988 film *Eight Men Out*. The film was produced by Sarah Pillsbury and Midge Sanford and is based on the book of the same name written by Eliot Asinof in 1962. After I first viewed the home video of the film, I was immediately convinced that it is little more than a huge over-dramatization of the 1919 World Series that has damaged the accuracy of the historical events that occurred. Perhaps several million people or so have viewed the film since its debut in 1988. These are persons who were not even remotely familiar with the 1919 World Series, the players or events and are now walking around with simplistic notions in their heads believing that what they saw portrayed in the film represented a factual account. Furthermore, I'm convinced that the film has done more to perpetuate myths and blatant misrepresentations of facts about the 1919 World Series than all of the five hundred articles that I have read combined.

Almost immediately, the film's assault on historical accuracy begins, with the White Sox players lethargically returning to the clubhouse from the field following their clinching of the 1919 American League pennant, only to find that penny-pinching owner Charles A. Comiskey has bestowed upon them an offering of stale champagne with which to toast their victory. Now this event did occur. It happened, however, two years prior, following the White Sox clinching of the 1917 American League pennant, not the 1919 pennant.

I suppose though that the most prominent myth acted out in the film is the totally misguided notion advanced by the producers that the 1919 Chicago White Sox were simply an invincible team. So invincible that they could only be beaten by a bunch of conniving gamblers collaborating with squirrelly little cheating ball players like Chick Gandil and certainly not the National League Champion Cincinnati Reds. This same simplistic notion of the powerful White Sox succumbing to the evils of gamblers' influence while ignoring the capabilities of the Reds is duplicated time and time again in every possible presentation of the 1919 World Series, from Ken Burns' 1994 PBS series *Baseball*, to even quasi-scholarly articles published by the Baseball Hall of Fame in its 1984 Fiftieth Anniversary book. To paraphrase the words of comedian Rodney Dangerfield, "The 1919 Cincinnati Reds get no respect."

Well, more than eight decades have passed since those controversial events of October 1919 were played out at Redland Field and Comiskey Park. Therefore, in my opinion it's high time to finally take an objective look at the players, managers, owners and actual events on the field to determine what is fact and what is myth regarding the outcome of the 1919 World Series.

It is not my intention to concentrate on the conspiracy theory in this book, as there already exists a mountain of literature on the subject for any interested reader. Nonetheless, in order to come up with a thorough and competent analysis of the 1919 World Series, one cannot just ignore the conspiracy elements. It will be necessary, therefore, from time to time to mention certain well-known but loosely documented events that occurred during the series which suggest questionable behavior on the part of a few Chicago players.

I do not take issue with sufficient evidence that suggests the 1919 World Series was spotted with some obviously shady goings-on and occasional lack of effort by a few White Sox players. Certainly the efforts of pitchers Eddie Cicotte and Charles "Lefty" Williams, first basemen Chick Gandil, and perhaps right fielder Happy Felsch are suspect.

However, the actual results of the series show that some of the White Sox players indicted in the conspiracy played very well and played to win. Shoeless Joe Jackson, who just happened to hit .375 in the series, said in an interview the year before he died in 1950 at the age of 62, "I played my heart out in that series." Another alleged conspirator, third baseman Buck Weaver, hit .324.

As for shabby play by the White Sox, well the record shows that for the eight games of the series both the White Sox and the Reds made 12 errors.

However, the primary motivation for this book is to re-examine the most prominent myth that has grown out of the 1919 World Series, the one that has elevated the 1919 Chicago White Sox to a team of superhuman status and by doing so has left the fact of just how good a team the 1919 Cincinnati Reds really were lost in a historical abyss.

Popular beliefs and myths aside, I will never be convinced that suspicious play of a few White Sox players is just cause to completely ignore the superior playing abilities of the Reds as a team. With or without a conspiracy to throw games by a few of the White Sox players, an informed baseball fan, after looking at both the statistics and actual events of the series, will come away as I did, convinced beyond a doubt that the Cincinnati Reds would have won the 1919 World Series without any help from their opponents. The record clearly shows the Cincinnati Reds were an excellent team capable of playing well with any club in either the National or American Leagues in 1919.

Pat Moran, the Reds' manager in 1919, swore that the Reds were a better team than the White Sox until the day he died prematurely at the age of 48 on March 7, 1924.

It's pointless to debate whether the 1919 Chicago White Sox were, as they are often referred to, the "best team ever assembled." Neither do I find it necessary to overly aggrandize the 1919 Cincinnati Reds. They were a very good team and so were the 1919 New York Giants and the 1919 Chicago Cubs.

I have taken an unbiased approach in looking back at the 1919 World Series and have set forth the historical events with neutrality. I urge readers to arrive at their own conclusions as to what is baseball fact and what has evolved into baseball myth. Thereby it is my intention to limit my opinions and present the relevant facts of this highly controversial event in major league baseball history.

CHAPTER ONE

Prelude to the 1919 World Series

The state of the national pastime in 1918 America was most precarious with American troops mired down in the trenches of France fighting World War I. Subsequently in May 1918 the United States government through General Enoch Crowder issued a general "work or fight" order. As a result, baseball was declared a nonessential endeavor in support of the war effort.

Players drafted or enlisting in the armed services suddenly depleted major-league rosters. The Detroit Tigers led the way, having 25 members of their organization answer the call to arms. In the National League the Brooklyn Robins and Pittsburgh Pirates sent 18 members of their organizations into the armed services. Hank Gowdy, the Boston Braves catcher, was the first major leaguer to enlist. In all, 247 players from major league rosters eventually served in World War I and 3 were listed as casualties.

In order to expedite the war effort in 1918, Labor Day, Monday, September 2, was designated as the end of the season. Therefore, as the abbreviated season came to an end, many of the game's most prominent stars marched off to war. Ty Cobb, Rabbit Maranville, Eppa Rixey, Casey Stengel and Grover Cleveland Alexander were among the first to enlist. St. Louis Cardinal executive Branch Rickey enlisted in the army and was commissioned a major.

The Cincinnati Reds sent just six members of their organization off to war, but one among them was manager Christy Mathewson, who

5

enlisted at the age of 37 and was commissioned a captain. Mathewson served in France and suffered gas poisoning, which is believed to have led to the tuberculosis that ended his life at age 45 in 1925. Former Reds infielder Eddie Grant (1911–1913) was killed in action at Argonne, France, on May 5, 1918.

The 1918 World Series began on Thursday, September 5, between the American League Champion Boston Red Sox and the National League Champion Chicago Cubs. The series' first game took place in Chicago (at Comiskey Park) and saw Red Sox pitcher Babe Ruth (13-7) lockup in a pitchers' duel with Cubs ace James "Hippo" Vaughn (22-10), in which Ruth and the Red Sox prevailed 1-0. The Red Sox then went on to win the series 4-2. However, while never substantiated, there were widespread reports circulating that the 1918 World Series had been fixed.

When the armistice was signed ending World War I on November 11, 1918, baseball owners became concerned about what effect a weakened postwar economy would have on baseball. Furthermore, rumors of gambling and bribes of major league players were rampant. If all those concerns weren't bad enough, influenza had just swept across the country in 1918, killing an estimated 548,000 people in the United States. During the 128-game suspended 1918 season, baseball saw just three million fans go through its turnstiles.

With the uncertainty of fan interest looming for the 1919 season, the owners agreed to schedule a 140-game season. However the owners' anxiety proved to be unfounded. Fan interest was never better, with total attendance rising to 6.5 million.

In the National League the New York Giants and Cincinnati Reds remained locked in a close race for first place most of the season. As a result attendance in New York jumped from 250,000 in 1918 to over 700,000 in 1919. In Cincinnati attendance tripled over the previous season as the Reds overtook John McGraw's Giants in early August for first place, then went on to clinch the pennant in mid-September. The Reds under the leadership of manager Pat Moran ultimately won the 1919 National League flag by nine games over the Giants, finishing with a 96-44 record.

Despite the fact that the Reds won the pennant by nine games, there were people then as there are today, who were so mean spirited about the Reds winning the 1919 World Series they attempted to deny them a legitimate National League pennant in 1919.

Now, those convinced that the Cincinnati Reds' win over the mighty Chicago White Sox in the 1919 World Series was a result of a conspiracy without objection also theorize that the Reds' win over the Giants in the National League pennant was tainted.

There were rumors and suspicions around the National League that two Giants players, first baseman Hal Chase and third baseman Heinie Zimmerman, were purposely making errors in the field that were hurting the Giants' pennant chances. Consequently, late in the 1919 season, manager John McGraw benched them.

Following the 1919 season Chase and Zimmerman were given lifetime banishment from baseball for attempting to bribe players to throw games. Later manager John McGraw was to suggest that the questionable play of Hal Chase and Heinie Zimmerman helped the Reds win the 1919 National League pennant over the Giants.

Unfortunately the fact that McGraw quickly forgot and the conspiracy advocates ignore is that the knockout blow the Reds delivered to the Giants in the 1919 National League pennant race came in August when they beat them in two crucial series. One of these series was played in the Polo Grounds too.

As for Hal Chase, following his banishment from the major leagues, he simply moved his act to the Pacific League where it is alleged that he continued to participate in some shady goings-on. Chase had won the National League batting title playing for the Reds in 1916 with an average of .316. An anomaly, Chase remains the only left-hand throwing and right-hand hitting player to ever win a major league batting title. Chase, who had been suspended by the Reds in 1918 after attempting to bribe an opposing pitcher, was traded to the Giants on February 2, 1919, for catcher Bill Rariden.

Heinie Zimmerman was previously suspended by the Giants in September 1918 after he offered a teammate, pitcher Rube Benton, $800 to throw a game.

Also, Zimmerman and Bill Rariden are both well-known for a botched rundown play in game six of the 1917 World Series between the New York Giants and Chicago White Sox. The play occurred in the fourth inning, the score 0-0 with Eddie Collins on third and Joe Jackson on first, when White Sox batter Happy Flesch grounded to pitcher Rube Benton. As Collins broke from third, Benton threw the ball to Zimmerman, who ran Collins toward the plate. However, Collins darted around catcher Bill Rariden who had left the plate unattended, and then Zimmerman chased Collins across the plate. This was the first run in a White Sox rally that saw them score three runs in the fourth as Chick Gandil then followed with a two-run single off Benton. The White Sox went on to win the game 4-2 and eventually win the World Series 4-2.

Over in the American League, the White Sox were in a three team race with the Cleveland Indians and New York Yankees until July 9 when they took the AL lead for good. The Indians continued to make a run at the White Sox throughout the summer until they wrapped up the pennant during late September in a game at St. Louis on a winning hit in the ninth inning by Joe Jackson.

Throughout the season the White Sox had been in a bitter salary struggle with owner Charles Comiskey, as they felt collectively short-changed in comparing their salaries against those of their American League counterparts. At one point the White Sox players asked manager Kid Gleason to intervene on their behalf with Comiskey. When Gleason did so and came back empty handed, it intensified the negative feelings between the White Sox players and Comiskey.

Final Standings 1919

National League					American League				
team	won	lost	pct.	GB	team	won	lost	pct.	GB
Cincinnati	96	44	.686		Chicago	88	52	.629	
New York	87	53	.621	9	Cleveland	84	55	.604	3.5
Chicago	75	65	.536	21	New York	80	59	.576	7.5
Pittsburgh	71	68	.511	24.5	Detroit	80	60	.571	8
Brooklyn	69	71	.493	27	St. Louis	67	72	.482	20.5
Boston	57	82	.410	38.5	Boston	66	71	.482	20.5
St. Louis	54	83	.394	40.5	Washington	56	84	.400	32
Philadelphia	47	90	.343	47.5	Philadelphia	36	104	.257	52

Team Batting 1919

National League		American League	
Cincinnati	.263	Chicago	.287
New York	.269	Cleveland	.278
Chicago	.256	New York	.267
Pittsburgh	.249	Detroit	.283
Brooklyn	.263	St. Louis	.264
Boston	.253	Boston	.261
St. Louis	.256	Washington	.260
Philadelphia	.251	Philadelphia	.244

In 1919 the Chicago White Sox were owned by Charles Albert Comiskey, also known in baseball circles as "Chommy" or "The Old Roman." Comiskey had played major league baseball for 13 years

(1882–1894) in the American Association with the St. Louis Browns and in the National League with the Cincinnati Reds. Chommy was a respectable player too, playing primarily at first base. In 1883, playing in 125 games for St. Louis, Comiskey hit .335. He finished his career having played in 1,390 games with a .261 lifetime batting average and getting 1,531 hits.

After his playing career ended, Comiskey remained in baseball and purchased the old Sioux City franchise, then moved it to Chicago in 1900. By all accounts, Comiskey developed a widely known reputation as a penny-pinching owner. The 1919 White Sox were underpaid by the salary standards of the day. While Ty Cobb was making $20,000 a year in Detroit, batting title rival Joe Jackson was making $6,000 a year playing for Comiskey in Chicago. Also it is historically reported that the White Sox had the lowest meal allowance in the major leagues.

One of the more popular episodes of Comiskey's penny-pinching habits is the Eddie Cicotte incident. Comiskey had promised Cicotte a raise in salary if the White Sox's pitching ace won 30 games in the 1919 season. With a week to go in the season Cicotte had won 29 games, then Comiskey ordered manager Kid Gleason to hold him out of the pitching rotation. However, in all fairness to Comiskey and Kid Gleason another factor in the decision to hold Cicotte out of the rotation during the final week of the season is usually overlooked.

Christy Mathewson, now out of the army and out of baseball as well, was hired by the *New York Times* to write a series of articles during the 1919 World Series and also describe the games as they were played. On September 30, 1919, the day before the series began, Mathewson wrote that pitching was going to be the most important factor in the series. He also stated that Eddie Cicotte might not be fit for the series, because the Chicago star had to work hard up to the final week of the season, while the Reds twirlers had rest.[1]

Whether Comiskey sensed that Cicotte needed to be rested the final week of the season to be at peak performance level for the World Series is at least debatable.

Nonetheless, with 5,577,496 fans going through Comiskey's turnstiles the White Sox had been the most successful franchise financially in the major leagues in the decade between 1910 and 1919. In fact, Charles Comiskey had called 1919 "The greatest season of all."

The Cincinnati Reds were owned in 1919 by yeast manufacturers Julius and Max Fleischmann, along with political bosses George B. Cox and August Gary Herrmann.

Herrmann, in addition to being the right-hand man sustaining Cox's

Eddie Cicotti baseball card for years 1912–1913 only. (Chicago Historical Society, SDN-U59678-C. Photography: *Chicago Daily News.* Cropped from left and right edges of original.)

political machine, by hiring and firing political cronies also allocated functions and framed the budgets for the City of Cincinnati. Also, Hermann was a powerful figure in the major leagues, serving with American League President Byron "Ban" Johnson and president of the National League Harry Pullian as head of the three-man National Baseball Commission that ruled baseball until 1921, when the owners hired Judge Kenesaw Mountain Landis as the first baseball commissioner in the aftermath of the suspicious activity during the 1919 World Series.

Herrmann had torn down Cincinnati's old inadequate ballpark "Palace of the Fans" built in 1884 and replaced it in 1912 with a new steel and concrete ballpark. In 1919 Redland Field, located at the corner of Western Avenue and York Street, was one of the most spacious parks in the major leagues with a center-field fence that was 420 feet from home plate and 360 feet down the left and right field lines. The first home run hit over the fence at Redland Field did not occur until 1921, when Reds outfielder Pat Duncan hit one over the left-field wall. That was one of only two home runs that Duncan belted in the 1921 season. Later in 1921 Babe Ruth, playing in an exhibition game, hit the first home run over the center-field fence at Redland Field.

Fan anticipation for the 1919 World Series was very high. Having misjudged the fan support for baseball in 1919 with the 140-game schedule, the baseball club owners were now eager to recoup some of the money by extending the World Series to nine games.

In New York City it was advertised in the *Times* that for a fee of 25 cents fans could see every action of every player in the 1919 World Series enacted direct from a wire at the 69th Regiment armory hall grounds, 25th Street and Lexington Avenue.

By 1919 the World Series was old hat to Chicago baseball fans. Since the World Series first began in 1903 there had already been six fall classics played in the windy city. The 1906 World Series, the third was an inter-city series between the Cubs and White Sox won by the Sox 4-2. Following the 1906 contest, the Cubs would appear in the World Series in 1907, 1908, 1910 and 1918. The White Sox would next play in the series in 1917 and, of course, were about to participate in the 1919 series.

However, the Cincinnati Reds and their fans were about to experience the excitement of the World Series for the very first time in the Queen City. Gary Herrmann even built temporary seats in Redland Field behind the left-field wall on York Street and sold them for $3 each. Ironically, these temporary seats were the only left-field bleachers the park ever had.

Although the White Sox were considered the superior of the two teams by the sportswriters, when the team and individual player performances of the 1919 Reds and White Sox are compared, the statistics hardly reveal an invincible Chicago team. On the contrary, the Reds compare favorably in nearly every category with the White Sox. In reality the Reds and White Sox were much alike. They both had very strong pitching and were good-hitting ball clubs with the ability to score runs.

Individual Batting Averages 1919

Cincinnati		*Chicago*	
Eddie Roush	.321	Eddie Murphy	.486 (35 at bats)
Hennie Groh	.310	Joe Jackson	.351
Jake Daubert	.276	Eddie Collins	.319
Ivy Wingo	.273	Nemo Leibold	.302
Larry Kopf	.270	Buck Weaver	.296
Morrie Rath	.264	Fred McMullin	.294
Pat Duncan	.244	Chick Gandil	.290
Greasy Neale	.242	Ray Schalk	.282
Bill Rariden	.216	Shano Collins	.279
Sherry Magee	.215	Happy Felsch	.275
Rube Bressler	.206	Swede Risberg	.256

Team Leaders in Home Runs 1919

Cincinnati		Chicago	
Hennie Groh	5	Happy Felsch	7
Eddie Roush	4	Joe Jackson	7
Bressler and Daubert (tied)	2	Eddie Collins	4

Stolen Bases 1919

Team

Cincinnati 143   Chicago 150* league leader

Individual Leaders

Cincinnati — Greasy Neale 28   Chicago — Eddie Collins 33

Team Fielding Statistics 1919

	Cincinnati	Chicago
Team Fielding Ave.	.974* league leader	.969
Team Errors	152* league leader	176
Double Plays	98	116

Team Pitching Statistics 1919

	Cincinnati	Chicago
ERA	2.23	3.04
Complete Games	89	88
Shut-Outs	23	14

Individual Pitching Leaders, Won-Lost and ERA 1919

Cincinnati	W L	ERA	Chicago	W L	ERA
Slim Sallee	21-7	2.06	Eddie Cicotte	29-7	1.82
Hod Eller	20-9	2.39	Lefty Williams	23-11	2.64
Dutch Ruether	19-6	1.82	Dickie Kerr	13-7	2.88
Ray Fisher	14-5	2.17	Red Faber	11-9	3.83
Jimmy Ring	10-9	2.26	G. Lowdermilk	5-5	2.79
Dolf Luque	9-3	2.63	Roy Wilkinson	1-1	2.05

1919 National & American League Leaders
on the Reds and White Sox

Cincinnati

Eddie Roush, Batting Champion .321
Dutch Ruether, best winning percentage .760
Hod Eller, most strikeouts/9 innings 4.97

Chicago

Eddie Collins, most stolen bases 33
Eddie Cicotte, best winning percentage .860
Eddie Cicotte, most wins 29
Eddie Cicotte, most complete games 30
Eddie Cicotte, fewest walks/9 innings 1.4

Neither the 1919 Reds nor the White Sox were long-ball threats, even by the standards of the dead-ball era. The National League home run king for 1919 was the Philadelphia Phillies Gavvy Cravath who led the league with 12. Over in the American League the home run king for 1919 with 29 round trippers was the Red Sox's Babe Ruth. However, the 1920 season ushered in the era of the live ball. Consequently, Babe Ruth, playing his first year in a New York Yankee uniform, would hit 54 home runs.

September 30, 1919, was the day before the World Series was to begin in Cincinnati. As fans arrived in Cincinnati anticipation of the match-up between the Reds and White Sox was running rampant. Because of the crowded conditions that the swell of fans brought to the city, hotels and boarding houses were booked up. Consequently, it was officially announced that fans unable to find accommodations would be able to sleep on benches in Redland Field. They were assured police protection by the Cincinnati city fathers to guard against thieves as much as possible.

Rumors that the World Series was going to be fixed had been persisting for weeks. In fact, Reds pitcher Hod Eller had even received a bribe from an unknown source of $5,000 to throw a game, which he turned down. In an article published by the *Cincinnati Post* in 1997, Marc Hardin recounts a 1985 interview with the last surviving member of the 1919 Cincinnati Reds, Edd Roush, in regards to the Eller bribe.

"The gamblers tried to work on our pitcher, Hod Eller, but he squelched them," Roush said. Roush said he was present when Reds manager Pat Moran called in Eller and asked him if a gambler approached him.

"Sure did," Roush reported Eller as saying. "Showed me five $1,000 bills if I'd make sure we lost today's game."

Roush then reported Moran asking Eller: "What'd you say?" To which Roush said Eller responded: "I told him to get out of my sight. If I ever saw him again, I'd beat him up."[2]

The White Sox had arrived in Cincinnati and were checked into the Hotel Sinton at Fourth and Vine Streets where it has long been held that some rather bizarre activities took place the night before the first game. Up in the room of White Sox pitcher Eddie Cicotte, a meeting was taking place with seven White Sox players present (Cicotte, Lefty Williams, Chick Gandil, Swede Risberg, Happy Flesch, Buck Weaver and Fred McMullin) along with an ex-featherweight champion of the world turned gambler by the name of Abe Attell and a former major league pitcher by the name of Billy Burns.

Abe Attell was said to represent New York gambling figure Arnold Rothstein. Rothstein had recently been informed by Attell that a former Philadelphia fighter by the name of Billy Maharg and a former major league pitcher Billy Burns (1908-1912, 35-52)had met a few weeks before the World Series with Eddie Cicotte and Chick Gandil at the Ansonia Hotel in New York. Subsequently, Attell had allegedly told Rothstein that Cicotte and Gandil were willing to throw the World Series for $100,000. However, as $100,000 was a considerable sum in 1919, Maharg and Burns needed Rothstein's financing power to consummate the fix.

Rothstein allegedly turned down the offer relayed from Burns through Attell. However, Burns then spoke with Giants first basemen Hal Chase, who convinced Burns that he should attempt to meet with Rothstein personally. Burns did meet with Rothstein but was turned down, as Rothstein did not think that the fix was possible.

Nonetheless, Attell liked the scheme and decided to pursue a fix without Rothstein. Without speaking to Rothstein, he assured Burns that Rothstein would put up the $100,000. However, Rothstein allegedly became convinced, through a meeting with one of his partners Nat Evans, that the fix was possible and then decided to participate in a plan to payoff the players.

Subsequently, as soon as the White Sox won the American League pennant, Evans went to Chicago along with Joseph Sullivan and met with Chick Gandil. Sullivan had known Gandil for several years. Previously, during the 1919 season the two had met at the Hotel Buckminster in Boston. It was at that meeting that Gandil allegedly told Sullivan that he wanted the World Series fixed. Hence it is believed that Sullivan was the one who ultimately convinced Rothstein to put up the fix money.

That evening of September 30, 1919, in Eddie Cicotte's room at the Hotel Sinton in Cincinnati, Billy Burns introduced Abe Attell to the seven members of the White Sox as the man handling the money in the fix for Arnold Rothstein. Attell allegedly told the players that he had been told by Rothstein not to give them a lump sum payment of $100,000, but rather to stagger payments of $20,000 a game over the course of the five games needed to dump the nine-game series.

In addition, it is believed that Attell and the players discussed what games they would lose, but Attell told them that was their decision. The players decided to dump the first two games of the series with Cicotte and Lefty Williams scheduled to pitch. Also there is speculation that the players wanted to lose game three as well because they did not particularly care for Dickie Kerr who was scheduled to pitch. Then they would win the fourth game pitched by Cicotte. As for the money due the players, after each loss it was agreed that Billy Burns would pick up the money from Attell and bring it to the Hotel Sinton following the game. Over the years it has been accepted that Arnold Rothstein had told Attell to have Cicotte hit the first batter to signal that the fix was on.

Despite the lack of grand jury testimony, I take no issue with the events described above, as they are not relevant to the thesis advanced in this book. Regardless if Cicotte and his cohorts decided to dump games, the net effect of their poor sportsmanship had very little to do with the eventual outcome of the World Series.

Joe Jackson was not present at the meeting in Cicotte's hotel room on September 30. Jackson was down in Charles Comiskey's room pleading with Chommy to keep him out of the starting lineup for game one. Jackson, who roomed with Lefty Williams on the road, had heard rumors of a fix and did not want to be part of it. He urged Comiskey to say that he had been drunk and was being held out of the starting lineup. It has been stated that Hugh Fullerton, a New York sportswriter, was in Comiskey's room during Jackson's visit and heard the entire exchange. Whether Fullerton was actually in the room experiencing the alleged encounter between Jackson and Gleason is controversial and part of the myth surrounding the actual events of the series.

One of several blatant inaccuracies in the movie *Eight Men Out* takes place in regards to this matter, as in the movie we find "Shoeless Joe" Jackson sitting on the bench feigning illness before game one and pleading with White Sox skipper Kid Gleason to keep him out of the starting lineup.

In a *Cincinnati Post* article written by Bill Koch in 1987, Reds center fielder Edd Roush had this to say about the alleged fix in the series.

"They threw the first ballgame," Roush said. "But they didn't get their money after the first ballgame, so they went out and tried to win."[3]

Roush went on say that throwing games in those days was a common occurrence. Roush himself had played on teams that threw games, although he never threw a ball game. In fact he was never even approached as Hod Eller had been.

"They knew better than to ask me," Roush said. "I would have knocked the hell out of them. And they knew that too."

Nonetheless, the stage was set for the 1919 World Series. The *New York Times* printed an article on the morning of the first game, which may have been a harbinger of things to come. Below is an excerpt from that article.

In the final preliminary analysis of the world's series there is one vital factor which demands much consideration. It is the psychology of the game. In baseball there are two expressions. "He's a good money player," or "It's a good money club," which, when defined, means the player or club is able to meet a crucial test without suffering from stage fright or blowing up. A player may be one of the greatest natural players in the game, but his temperament may be such that it prevents him from meeting emergencies upon which much depend without having his playing seriously affected by nervousness. The player who in the pinches is able to perform is a "good money player." And nerves must be weighed in the balance as the Chicago White Sox and Cincinnati Reds parade to the post for the first game of the world's series in Cincinnati this afternoon. Will either of the teams blow? And if such a thing happened, which club will it be? Those are the important questions which present themselves at the eleventh hour.[4]

CHAPTER TWO

Game One

At Cincinnati, October 1, 1919

	1	2	3	4	5	6	7	8	9	R	H	E
Chicago	0	1	0	0	0	0	0	0	0	1	6	1
Cincinnati	1	0	0	5	0	0	2	1		9	14	1

Cicotte, Wilkinson (4), Lowdermilk (8)
Ruether

For a brief moment in the early autumn of 1919, the City of Cincinnati seemed to take center stage on all earthly events. Special trains had been run from Chicago and Pittsburgh bringing legions of fans—men, women and children—into Cincinnati for the World Series. Four hundred visiting and local newspapermen were on hand for the series. A reporter from the *Philadelphia Inquirer* asked Reds president August Gary Herrmann for a prediction on the series. Herrmann smiled and said, "I have been busy trying to keep some 150,000 fans from being sore because they can't be placed where there is room for only 33,000."[1]

At 10:00 AM the gates to Redland Field were opened and there was a tremendous rush by fans entering the park for the bleachers and pavilion where those arriving first would get the best seats in the front rows. As game time neared, Redland Field became packed with an overflow crowd of 30,511 anticipating the start of the series. In order to sell a few more tickets, August Gary Herrmann and the other Reds owners had constructed temporary bleachers over York Street. These seats sold for $3.00 each.

Scalpers with tickets to sell were everywhere and only one hour before the start of the game did they slash their prices to face value in an effort to cut their loses. Prior to that box seats for three games costing $10.80 were being sold at prices ranging from $40 to $100. A reporter saw one fellow pay $125 for three $5 tickets for game one.

In the buildings beyond the right and center field wall hundreds of others took up positions in windows and on the rooftops to view the game. Still other fans were hanging from telephone poles beyond the outfield wall for a view.

During batting practice fans in other temporary seats constructed in the outfield beneath the temporary bleachers raced to retrieve balls that went past outfielders. Cincinnati policemen were stationed at intervals around the barriers about five yards apart and stood by passively as fans jumped the barriers and ran on to the field to retrieve balls. Eventually, with balls going all over the outfield, the policemen themselves started to retrieve souvenirs. Youngsters became very amused when they beat the policemen in a foot race to retrieve a ball.

When the Chicago White Sox players came on the field for batting practice they put on quite a display of hitting. Sox third sacker Buck Weaver even cleared the left-field grandstand with a foul ball, which bounded on the roof of the stand in an adjoining street.

As game time neared, Redland Field Park Superintendent Matty Schwab had the diamond and outfield in pristine condition for the World Series. Schwab had even built a new scoreboard in right field for the series. Schwab would continue working at the ballpark, later renamed Crosley Field, for 69 years, retiring in 1963.

Eddie Cicotte, the White Sox ace who had a season record of (29-7), was the starting pitcher for Chicago. There had been a lot of speculation about the condition of Cicotte's arm the past couple of weeks leading up to the series. The press had been speculating that if it had not been for reports that Eddie Cicotte's arm was lame, the White Sox would be heavy favorites to win the series. No one knew for sure what the actual condition of Cicotte's arm really was. Nonetheless, he hadn't made many starts in the last few weeks and when he did, he was hit rather hard. With the question of Cicotte's arm outstanding, the White Sox, while 8-5 favorites to win the series, were 2-1 underdogs to win the first two games in Cincinnati.

For the Reds, manager Pat Moran selected southpaw Walter Dutch

Ruether as the starting pitcher. Ruether had pitched mainly in the western leagues and been branded a cast off by the minor leagues. He had pitched for Kansas City and Salt Lake and Spokane had even offered him for $300 to any taker in the draft. He was drafted by the Chicago Cubs in 1917 and was unable to finish one game. Prior to 1919 Ruether had only won three games in the majors. However, during the Reds' march to the National League Championship in 1919, he achieved an outstanding season record of 19-6. Pat Moran's strategy seemed to be that if he could win game one with Ruether, then he had five other very good starters to fall back on — Slim Sallee, Hod Eller, Jimmy Ring, Ray Fisher and Dolf Luque.

Moran had said in a press conference the day before, "We will play as well as we did to win the pennant. That means we will put up the hardest kind of a fight. The Cincinnati players realize that they are going up against a great ball club, but they are not the least bit worried."[2]

"I have told them that Cicotte and Williams can be defeated. Our pitchers in my opinion can prevent nearly all the White Sox from hitting when bases are occupied. If we beat Cicotte in the first game we ought to win the series, because the other Chicago pitchers will lose some of their confidence. All of the games should be close and I hope we get the breaks."

White Sox manager Kid Gleason had a different prediction on the series. "Why there's nothing to it. I said last June that the Sox would win the pennant even with only Cicotte and Williams in the box. My ball club will beat the Reds without being greatly extended. Why? Because we have the greatest hitting team that ever played for the title. The Reds have some good pitchers, but they can't stop us."[3]

Gleason refused to acknowledge reports of Cicotte's questionable arm and with Urban Red Faber (who had won three games in the 1917 World Series against the New York Giants) ill and out for the series, he was spread pretty thin pitching wise, having just Lefty Williams and rookie Dickie Kerr as healthy starting pitchers. Consequently, Gleason was confronted with the thought of having to face a Reds team with six starting pitchers and that had a season ERA of 2.23 in 1919, second best in the National League, better than Chicago's team ERA of 3.04 and in fact better than every team ERA in the American League.

Nonetheless, prior to the game Kid Gleason is said to have had a clubhouse meeting with his players in which he addressed the rumors of the White Sox purposely losing games in the series. Gleason is supposed to have said, "Now, I've heard that some of you fellows have arranged to throw the series." Eighty-plus years of legend and retelling of this story in various versions has it that in reaction to Gleason's remarks, some players looked bewildered, while other just kept their heads down and stared at the clubhouse floor.

The Starting Lineups for Game One

Cincinnati	Chicago
Rath, 2b	J. Collins, rf
Daubert, 1b	E. Collins, 2b
Groh, 3b	Weaver, 3b
Roush, cf	Jackson, lf
Duncan, lf	Felsch, cf
Kopf, ss	Gandil, 1b
Neale, rf	Risberg, ss
Wingo, c	Schalk, c
Ruether, p	Cicotte, p

Prior to the start of the game, a small airplane flew above Redland Field and dropped bunches of fluttering advertising circulars all over the infield and outfield. Matty Schwab's grounds crew, upset and gesturing at the airplane, retrieved them.

Umpire Jimmy Rigler took his position behind the plate as Dutch Ruether took the mound and then tossed about a half dozen warm-up pitches. White Sox leadoff batter John "Shano" Collins stepped up to the plate, and the 1919 World Series was underway.

Ruether survived the first inning against the mighty White Sox with ease. He got behind on John "Shano" Collins two balls and one strike before Shano lined a single into center. However, Shano was tagged out at second after Eddie Collins attempted to sacrifice. Eddie Collins then tested the arm of Reds catcher Ivy Wingo and was thrown out attempting to steal second base. Buck Weaver, who was at the plate when Collins attempted his mad dash for second, then hit Ruether's next pitch on a fly to left that was caught by Edd Roush, who dashed all the way from his position in center field to make the catch and the third out.

The Reds wasted no time drawing first blood in the series. Morrie Rath led off the bottom of the first inning and took Cicotte's first pitch for a strike. On the second pitch to Rath, Cicotte hit him squarely in the back. This of course was supposed to be the infamous signal from Cicotte to the gamblers that the fix of the series was in. Jake Daubert then followed with a single over second base into right center, sending Rath to third. The Cincinnati fans were ecstatic over the early trouble Cicotte found himself in and cheered wildly as Reds Captain Heinie Groh stepped up to the plate. Groh then hit a long fly to left into the waiting hands of Joe Jackson as Rath then tagged up from third and dashed home with the Reds' first run of the series.

The White Sox came back quickly in the top of the second inning and tied the score at 1-1. Joe Jackson led off by hitting a grounder behind second that Kopf the shortstop knocked down, fumbled and threw wild to first base. The ball wound up in the crowd behind the Reds' dugout allowing Jackson to sprint to second on the wild toss. Happy Felsch then laid down a sacrifice on the first pitch and Jackson moved over to third. Chick Gandil followed, lifting a short fly ball into left; however, the Reds' infield was playing in on the grass and the outfield too far out. Nonetheless, Edd Roush made a fine effort to field the ball, but it dropped in and Jackson scored.

Cicotte then settled down and pitched good ball the next two innings, permitting just one base runner when he walked Dutch Ruether to open up the bottom of the third. Likewise for Dutch Ruether. He set the Sox down in order in both the third and fourth.

The October 2, 1919, edition of the *New York Times* states that as Cicotte took the field for the fourth inning "[He] seemed apprehensive as he took the mound for this frame. He scanned the field minutely and gave the outfielders particular attention."[4] In fact, Cicotte's apprehension would become immediate terror as the hard-hitting Reds would drive him from the mound, scoring five runs in the inning.

After Edd Roush flied out to deep center, Pat Duncan followed by lining the next pitch over Eddie Collins' head into right for a single. Larry Kopf then hit a bounder back to Cicotte who quickly fielded the ball, but momentarily hesitated before he threw to Risberg forcing Duncan at second. However, after taking the throw from Cicotte, Risberg stumbled over the bag and Kopf beat his throw to first in the attempted double play.

With two outs and Kopf on first, the Reds opened the floodgates on Cicotte. Greasy Neale hit the ball hard through the box over second base. Kopf took second on the hit. Ivy Wingo then hit a liner into right for a single, scoring Kopf. Neale took third and Wingo took second on a belated throw by Shano Collins to the plate in an attempt to get Kopf. Dutch Ruether then crashed the ball into a temporary fence in left center for a triple, scoring Neale and Wingo.

The White Sox infield then had a conference with Cicotte on the mound. Morrie Rath then came up to bat and hit the ball past the outstretched arms of Buck Weaver at third into left, scoring Ruether with the fourth run of the inning. Rath took second on the throw to home. Jake

Cincinnati Reds, 1919. Top row (left to right): Magee, Roush, Rath, Eller, Sallee, Garner, Fisher, Ring and Groh. Middle row (left to right): Daubert, See, Ruether, Moran, Rariden, Allen, Wingo, Neale, Bressler. Bottom row (left to right): Smith, Luque, Duncan, Kopf, Mitchell and bat boy. (Cincinnati Museum Center Photograph Archives.)

Daubert then ran the count to three balls and one strike before stroking a single into right center, scoring Rath with the Reds' fifth run of the inning. Daubert, playing heads-up ball, became the second base runner of the inning to take second on a throw home by Shano Collins.

At this point Kid Gleason stormed the mound and waived Cicotte from the game. Cicotte then walked to the dugout with his head bowed. The highly partisan Reds crowd went wild with joy at the complete humiliation of the White Sox ace. Gleason brought in twenty-five-year-old rookie Roy Wilkinson to pitch, who finally got the Reds out as Heinie Groh flied out to Happy Felsch to end the inning.

Ruether, now with a commanding 6-1 lead, handled the Sox with ease through the next three innings, allowing no runs and just three hits.

In the bottom of the seventh the Reds would add two more insurance runs. Jake Daubert would lead off against Wilkinson with a ground-rule triple after his drive to right bounced into the crowd. Heinie Groh then hit a ball that caromed off Wilkinson's glove and passed Risberg, scoring Daubert from third with the Reds' seventh run. Roush then laid down a bunt along the third-base line for a sacrifice and was safe at first on a bad throw by Weaver. Roush, hard charging down the first-base line, knocked the ball from Gandil's glove as he collided with him upon reaching the bag. Groh then dashed for third and slid in ahead of Gandil's throw. The White Sox infield then moved in. Pat Duncan hit a grounder to short that Swede

Risberg fielded and shoveled off to Eddie Collins, forcing Roush at second base. However, Groh scored by beating Eddie Collins' throw to the plate, giving the Reds an 8-1 lead in the game.

Grover Lowdermilk became the third Chicago pitcher in the bottom of the eighth entering the game after Fred McMullin had pinch-hit for Roy Wilkinson in the top of the eighth. The Reds scored their ninth run of the game off Lowdermilk as Greasy Neale singled to left. Ivy Wingo sacrificed Neale to second, then Dutch Ruether smashed his second triple of the game off the center field fence, scoring Neale.

In the top of the ninth Ruether retired Jackson, Felsch and Gandil in order, giving the Reds a 9-1 victory in the first game of the series.

It certainly was Dutch Ruether's day as he had a relatively easy time defeating the White Sox, throwing just 88 pitches while giving up one run and six hits. Furthermore, at bat he had a single, two triples and walked once. Seldom has a pitcher then or now ever been as dominating a force in a World Series game as Ruether was in game one. In fact, Sox manager Kid Gleason remarked, "Ruether had a world of stuff today and pitched a remarkable game. His batting stamps him as the second Babe Ruth."[5]

Jim Nasium, writing in the *Philadelphia Inquirer* following game one, stated, "Probably fifty-nine years from now the old boys will be telling the young fellows that they were there when Pat Moran's Reds humbled the mighty White Sox from Chicago by the tune of 9 to 1, and will be recounting how one Dutch Ruether banged out a pair of triples and a single and won his own ball game."[6]

For more than eight decades now, the loss of game one by the White Sox has been blamed on the lackluster pitching of Eddie Cicotte by most of the conspiracy theory devotees and legions of uniformed fans that have evolved since the event took place. However, the facts of the game show that in the critical fourth inning it was not Cicotte's brief hesitation but rather the bad relay throw by Swede Risberg to Chick Gandil that failed to complete the double play on Morrie Rath that did the real damage. Had Risberg completed that double play, Cicotte would have been out of the inning without giving up a run and would have probably completed the game. Instead the Reds scored five runs.

As for Cicotte's pitch that hit Morrie Rath in the first inning, Ken Burns and Geoffrey C. Ward in their 1994 PBS documentary *Baseball* conclude that the fix in the series was visible from the first pitch. Actually Cicotte's first pitch to Rath was a strike. However, the instant fix theory is really an unfortunate broad generalization on the part of Burns and Ward. There was no video tape in 1919 and the movie technology that existed was still primitive and unable to document a play by play account of the series. Nonetheless, it is heavily documented that the 1919 World Series was to be in reality a very exciting World Series, one that broke all previous gate receipt records and that was intensified with some brilliant pitching and very skillful play on the field by both the Reds and White Sox.

Burns and Ward were making a disjointed documentary film and needed to generalize, rather than analyze, the events of the 1919 World Series as much as possible to allow them to move rapidly their main agenda, which was a big lead in to the Babe Ruth era. In doing so they left a huge gap in their credibility as historians

Kid Gleason, referring to Cicotte's early exit in the game, stated, "When Cicotte hit Rath in the first inning he was not himself thereafter. I could have taken him out then, but I trusted that luck would enable Eddie to regain his control."[7]

But the fact of the matter is that in their stunning 9-1 victory in game one the Reds had 14 hits and showed a lot more hustle than the White Sox. Not only did Ruether have three hits, but Greasy Neale and Jake Daubert did as well. Edd Roush stole a base. Also Roush, Morrie Rath, Ivy Wingo and Heinie Groh completed successful sacrifices. The Reds took the extra base when the opportunity presented itself too, twice taking extra bases following throws to the plate by Shano Collins that ultimately resulted in runs and once following a throw to the plate by Eddie Collins that also resulted in a run.

The White Sox on the other hand did not have an extra-base hit and left five men on base. Even if Eddie Cicotte, the pride of the American League, did not have a sore arm or was not in on an alleged conspiracy, this game was not going to be won by the Sox. This first-ever World Series game to be played in Cincinnati was simply destined to be won by the Reds.

Christy Mathewson reported in his article for the *New York Times* following the game, "That is the kind of baseball I like to see, because it was an attack against the best pitcher Chicago is supposed to have. It showed that they were not afraid to go right out after the pitching. They were not hesitating. After the game I saw Tris Speaker. He said, 'Cicotte's last three games in the regular season had been bad, and this is his fourth.' I want to make a prediction. If as Speaker says, Cicotte has not the stuff he carried through the season, it appears as if Moran's Reds will win in seven games at the outside. I never bet on a ball game, but if we get another warm day tomorrow and Sallee starts for Cincinnati, I think I will get down a little wager on the Reds."[8]

Apparently a lot of fans felt the same way as Mathewson. Before game one the White Sox were 8-5 favorites to win the series; following game one the Reds had suddenly become 7-10 favorites to win the World Series.

Game one was a huge success at the gate too, with total receipts of $98,778.00.

Later that evening back at the Hotel Sinton, it is documented that Kid Gleason confronted some of his players in the lobby in front of a large gathering of spectators. One version of this story has Gleason confronting Swede Risberg, Eddie Cicotte, Chick Gandil and Joe Jackson. Another version of the incident has Gleason confronting just Cicotte and Gandil, because they seemed to be in such good spirits following a game in which they took a pounding. Regardless of which version is accurate, if either, it is not really known if Gleason's outburst at the players was in reaction to their play (or lack of play) that day, or whether it was in further reference to any rumors of a conspiracy. Kid Gleason, a tough competitor, was mad as hell about the opening-game loss and did not care to lose in any circumstance, much less in an atmosphere of conspiracy rumors.

Box Score Game One

Chicago	ab	r	h	rbi	Cincinnati	ab	r	h	rbi
J. Collins, rf	4	0	1	0	Rath, 2b	3	2	1	1
E. Collins, 2b	4	0	1	0	Daubert, 1b	4	1	3	1
Weaver, 3b	4	0	1	0	Groh, 3b	3	1	1	2
Jackson, lf	4	1	0	0	Roush, cf	3	0	0	0
Felsch, cf	3	0	0	0	Duncan, lf	4	0	2	1
Gandil, 1b	4	0	2	1	Kopf, ss	4	1	0	0
Risberg, ss	2	0	0	0	Neale, rf	4	2	3	0
Schalk, c	3	0	0	0	Wingo, c	3	1	1	1
Cicotte, p	1	0	0	0	Ruether, p	3	1	3	3
Wilkinson, p	1	0	0	0					
McMullin, ph	1	0	1	0					
Lowdermilk, p	0	0	0	0					

Chicago	ip	h	r	er	bb	so
Cicotte	3⅔	7	6	6	2	1
Wilkinson	3⅓	5	2	1	0	1
Lowdermilk	1	2	1	1	0	0

Cincinnati						
Ruether	9	6	1	0	1	1

LOB Cincinnati 7, Chicago 5, E Gandil 1, Kopf 1, 2B Rath, 3B Ruether 2, Daubert, S Felsch, Rath, Roush, Wingo, Groh, SB Roush, HBP Cicotte 1, Lowdermilk 1

CHAPTER THREE

Game Two

At Cincinnati, October 2, 1919

	1	2	3	4	5	6	7	8	9	R	H	E
Chicago	0	0	0	0	0	0	2	0	0	2	10	1
Cincinnati	0	0	0	3	0	1	0	0		4	4	2

Williams
Sallee

Cincinnati is a community well known for extremes in weather. In July it is normally as hot as New Orleans, and in January the climate conditions often mimic that of Fargo, North Dakota. For game two of the series the weather was rather warm in Cincinnati, but a tempering breeze prevented conditions from being oppressive.

But fan interest was boiling nonetheless. There was just as much enthusiasm about the series today as yesterday. However, fans had come to the realization that it was impossible for the Reds' ownership to put two persons in a space designed to accommodate one. The attendance of 29,600 for the second game was slightly less than that of the opening game. However, fans took up vantage points wherever they could to get a glimpse of the action. Up on the summit of Fairview Heights a crowd of more than fifty persons had gathered for a bird's-eye view of the action down at Redland Field.

Judge Kenesaw Mountain Landis, an ardent White Sox fan, was present for the games in Cincinnati as a guest of Cincinnati Judge Woodmansee.

The *Philadelphia Inquirer* had run a local contest in the City of Brotherly Love and fifty lucky winners dubbed the "Famous Fifty" were given an expense-paid trip to the World Series. The "Famous Fifty" for the most part were partisan supporters of the White Sox, having a loyalty connection with White Sox second baseman Eddie Collins who had played a significant role in Connie Mack's famous $100,000 infield that had won American League pennants in 1910, 1911, 1913 and 1914. Also White Sox manager Kid Gleason had been a pitcher for the Philadelphia Quakers/Phillies from 1885 to 1891, then an infielder for the Phillies from 1903 to 1908.

However, on the other hand Reds shortstop Larry Kopf had formerly played for the Athletics in 1914 and 1915 and Reds manager Pat Moran had played for the Phillies from 1910 to 1914. Then Moran became manager of the Phillies for four seasons (1915–1918), winning the National League pennant in 1915.

As the White Sox came on the field for pre-game practice, a brass band began playing the mournful ballad "She May Have Seen Better Days," popular in the late 1890s.

Pat Moran had been undecided about whether he would start Hod Eller or Slim Sallee in game two. In the end Moran gave the assignment to Sallee despite the fact that Sallee had faced the White Sox in the 1917 World Series while with the Giants and been beaten by them twice. But Sallee had a brilliant 1919 season with a 21-7 record and certainly deserved a chance at starting game two against the Sox despite his past history against them.

Not to anyone's surprise, Kid Gleason decided to go with Claude "Lefty" Williams in game two. In the regular season Williams had a record of 23-11.

The *New York Times* reported prior to game two:

> The victory in the first game with Chicago gave the supporters of the Reds all confidence in the world, and they were willing to dig deep into their coffers to back their favorites with real money. White Sox fans were figuring last night that Claude Williams would be Kid Gleason's choice today, and they figured that the lefthander might do better against the many port side hitters on the Cincinnati club than Cicotte did.
>
> With four left-handed hitters on the Reds (Rath, Daubert, Roush, Neale) followers of the American League champions were sanguine that Williams would be able to stop the Cincinnati onslaught. And this in spite of the fact that the Reds had proved to be a thoroughly efficient club against left-handed

pitching this season. The record shows that Cincinnati Club has been any-thing but a mark for southpaws. In a majority of instances left-handed pitch-ers have been roughly handled by Pat Moran's warriors.[1]

At 1:58 P.M., home plate umpire Bill Evans called out "Play ball," and White Sox leadoff hitter Shano Collins stepped up to the plate and took the first pitch from Sallee shoulder high for ball one. Collins then hit the second pitch, a weak grounder to the box where Sallee fielded the ball and threw to Daubert at first for the out. Sallee then walked Eddie Collins bringing up Buck Weaver. Weaver hit a sharp line drive to Kopf at short-stop, who then threw to first doubling up Collins.

In the bottom of the first, Reds leadoff hitter Morrie Rath stepped up to the plate and was greeted with prolonged applause by the home team fans. Rath then took Lefty Williams to a full count before flying out to Happy Felsch in center. Williams then finished up the inning quickly as Daubert grounded out and Reds Captain Heinie Groh lined the ball to right. Shano Collins made a remarkable play on the ball and was given a sustained cheer by Reds and White Sox fans as he ran off the field.

Joe Jackson led off the top of the second inning with a liner to cen-ter that just got by the hands of Edd Roush by inches. Happy Felsch then sacrificed, Sallee to Daubert. Jackson took third. Sallee then retired Gandil on a ground ball, Kopf to Daubert, and Risberg on a fly ball to Neale in right.

After Williams walked to Roush leading off in the bottom of the sec-ond, Pat Duncan hit a hard line drive into the glove of Eddie Collins who doubled up Roush at first. Lefty Williams then got Larry Kopf out on a high fly ball to Felsch in center.

In the top of third, Ray Schalk lined out to Roush in left center. Lefty Williams then got the White Sox's second hit off of Sallee by lining a sin-gle into center. However, Williams died at first as Shano Collins flied out to left and Eddie Collins was fooled by a slow ball from Sallee, grounding out to Daubert at first.

Williams then retired the Reds in order in the bottom of the third, keeping the pitchers' duel alive.

In the top of the fourth Buck Weaver led off hitting Sallee's first pitch into center for a single. Joe Jackson followed with a single into left. Pat Duncan, however, came in on the ball quickly and held Weaver to second. Happy Felsch laid down a sacrifice bunt and both runners advanced. Chick Gandil then swung at Sallee's first pitch and grounded to Daubert, who threw home to get Weaver by 12 feet.

An example of high profiled inaccurate research in regards to the play at the plate on Weaver appears in *Baseball, An Illustrated History*, the companion book to Ward and Burns' documentary. On pages 135 and 136 a full-page photo appears referenced as Buck Weaver being out at the plate by Cincinnati's Bill Rariden in game two. However, the photo was taken at Comiskey Park, not Redland Field, scene of the second game. The photo most probably is from the 1917 World Series between the New York Giants and White Sox. Rariden was the catcher for the 1917 Giants.

Continuing with the top of the fourth, Jackson was on third, Gandil on first and there were two outs. With Swede Risberg at the plate, Gandil broke for second and slid in safe, with Rariden making no attempt to throw him out. Risberg took Sallee to a full count then hit a pop fly to Daubert at first, ending the inning.

In the bottom of the fourth the pitchers' duel between Williams and Sallee came to an end. Morrie Rath led off with a walk, and the crowd began to cheer as he took first base. Jake Daubert then laid down a sacrifice bunt and was thrown out, Williams to Gandil. With Rath on second Williams walked Groh. Ray Schalk and Chick Gandil then held a conference on the mound with Williams. Next up was Edd Roush, the 1919 National League batting champion, who connected against Williams and drove the ball over second, into center. Rath dashed for home from second scoring ahead of the throw from Felsch. Groh took third. Pat Duncan had worked Williams to a full count when Roush attempted to steal second and was thrown out by Ray Schalk. Duncan then took ball four from Williams. Larry Kopf then hit the first pitch from Williams into the temporary fence in left field for a triple, scoring Groh from third and Duncan from first. Williams finally got out the inning when Greasy Neale grounded out, Eddie Collins to Gandil.

The Reds scored three runs in the fourth inning and the damage was done. The White Sox would not catch up despite continuing to get hits off Sallee throughout the remainder of the game.

In the top of the fifth Sallee retired the White Sox in order.

Bill Rariden led off for the Reds in the bottom half of the fifth and hit a single into deep left field along the foul line. Joe Jackson, who is often criticized unfairly for his fielding in the series by those advancing the conspiracy theory, made a great stop on the ball. Slim Sallee, after two failed attempts to sacrifice and fouling off a few other of Williams' pitches, flied out to Felsch in center. Rath then hit a pop fly just outside the infield. Risberg attempted to field the ball but wound up juggling it, even attempting a shoestring catch as the ball rolled between his legs, allowing Rath to reach first and Rariden to take second. Williams, however, got out of the inning unscathed as Daubert popped out to Eddie Collins and Groh lined out to Felsch.

Eddie Collins led off for the White Sox in the top of the sixth and lined out to Kopf. Buck Weaver then stepped into one of Sallee's pitches and lined the ball over Pat Duncan's head in left into the temporary stands for a double. Sallee then fanned Jackson and the crowd cheered wildly as Shoeless Joe walked away from the plate. Sallee then balked and umpire Evans moved Weaver to third. Happy Felsch followed with a long fly to center. Edd Roush ran almost all the way to the wall to make a fabulous leaping catch! As Roush pulled the ball in for the third out, both fans in the stands and those watching the action up on the hilltop in Fairview Heights were seen doing the snake dance.

Cincinnati police Night Chief of Detectives Emmet Kirgan, commenting on the action up on Fairview Heights, told a reporter that the fans up there "Must have the eye of an eagle and I'm sure they've got a bird's eye view."[2]

As Roush walked up to the plate to lead off the bottom of the sixth, the fans greeted him with a thundering ovation. Williams walked Roush. This was his second pass of the game. Duncan then laid down a sacrifice Williams to Gandil, moving Roush to second. Kopf then fouled out to Weaver. Greasy Neale then singled into left, scoring Roush with the Reds' fourth run of the game. With Rariden up, Neale then attempted to steal second and was thrown out, Schalk to Risberg.

Before the White Sox came up to bat in the top of the seventh, once again for the second day in a row a low-flying airplane appeared over the park. So low flying in fact that it seemed only a few feet above the grandstand roof. As it flew over the diamond, a figure appeared to lean forward from its seat and all at once fell out crashing to the ground near third base. Chick Gandil had just come up to bat and play was momentarily stopped. Many lady spectators were extremely alarmed. However, a Cincinnati policeman came forth and grabbed the would-be victim and carried if off the field. It was a dummy and the policeman utilized it as a comfortable seat for the rest of the afternoon.

Herein lies one of the most exaggerated events of the 1919 World Series. Hollywood provided a distorted version of this event in the film *Eight Men Out* as some sort of an ominous sign of the White Sox skullduggery in throwing games in the series. But more than likely the entire incident was nothing more than an attempt by an overzealous Reds fan attempting to symbolically state his opinion that the White Sox were already defeated in the World Series. In short, the Sox were dead. To this day, there has not been one iota of evidence that even remotely suggests that this incident was anything more, much less a threatening message to the White Sox players regarding a conspiracy.

World Series. Second game at Cincinnati. Neale out stealing 2nd base. White Sox lost game 4-2. Cincinnati, OH. (Chicago Historical Society SDN-061956. Cropped from bottom edge of original.)

Play was resumed and Chick Gandil grounded out, Daubert to Sallee. Sallee then lost his bid for a shutout as Swede Risberg followed with a line single to left. Ray Schalk then hit the ball down the right-field line, rounded first quickly and stretched his hit into a double. Neale's poor throw to second took a bad bounce and got by both Rath and Kopf. Groh was covering third and no one backed up the play. Consequently, the ball rolled into foul territory. Groh went after the ball like a deer and made an attempt to get the ball to Rariden, but his throw hit Schalk in the back. Both Risberg and Schalk scored. Sallee then ended the inning by striking out Williams and getting Shano Collins to fly out to Roush in center.

In the bottom of the seventh Lefty Williams set down the Reds in order.

Sallee handled the first two White Sox up in the top of the eighth with ease as Eddie Collins flied out to Roush and Buck Weaver grounded out, Kopf to Daubert. Joe Jackson then hit the ball hard to Daubert, but Sallee was late in covering first and Daubert's throw got by him. Jackson then rounded first and took second base on the error. Happy Felsch then almost knocked Groh over with a line shot too hot to hold. However, Groh recovered the ball and threw to Daubert for the third out.

Jake Daubert opened the home half of the eighth by grounding out,

Risberg to Gandil. Williams then walked Groh. Edd Roush then hit a twisting fly back of second that Happy Felsch made a great running catch on. Groh didn't think that Felsch could get to the ball and dashed for second, then seeing the ball caught, he attempted to get back to first. Felsch threw the ball to Eddie Collins who pegged it to Gandil at first, doubling up Groh.

In the top of the ninth the Sox continued to hit Sallee, but to no avail as Gandil singled to center. However, Risberg followed by hitting into a double play, Rath to Kopf to Daubert. Ray Schalk then ran the count full on Sallee before hitting a single into center. At that point Kid Gleason sent reserve infielder Fred McMullin up to pinch-hit for Williams. McMullin grounded out, Rath to Daubert, ending the game.

The White Sox outhit the Reds in the game 10-4, but were unable to bunch their hits into runs. The difference in the game was the bad control that Lefty Williams had in the fourth inning when he walked three and gave up two hits leading to three of the Reds' four runs. Overall Williams did not pitch such a bad game, he only allowed four hits, but he walked six, and four of those walks resulted in runs.

Slim Sallee, despite throwing only 92 pitches, was hit hard by the White Sox giving up ten hits. However, if it had not been for the bad throw by Greasy Neale to second base in the top of the seventh inning which allowed Risberg and Schalk to score, Sallee may have shutout the White Sox.

On the other hand Edd Roush saved a pair of runs when he made his spectacular catch of the ball hit to deep center by Happy Felsch in the top of the sixth. If that ball had gotten by Roush it would have gone for an inside-the-park home run and scored two runs. Therefore the score would have been 3-2 Reds at that point in the game and the Sox could have turned it all around.

The White Sox hit the ball hard, but time and time again their hits went directly towards a Reds fielder. Even White Sox skipper Kid Gleason called the Reds victory in the second game a lucky one. "We outhit them nearly three to one, but the breaks of the game went against us. The Sox are far from out of the race. We have the greatest comeback ball club in the world, and those two beatings will make my players fight all the harder to even it up. Williams showed today that the Reds hitting can be stopped, but he had an unfortunate inning in the fourth when he walked three men, the Reds' victory was almost given to them on a platter. They got four hits. We got ten hits. We'll outhit them in the series. Fielding that happens only once in a lifetime robbed us of enough runs to win. Roush is a marvel in the outfield and my players give him all the credit for his work."[3]

So the Reds were probably lucky to some extent to get away with a victory in game two. But the Reds showed character in making their hits count and making the big play when they needed it. That is the mark of a true championship ball club. Perhaps all those who have maintained that the Reds were badly outclassed by the White Sox, or as maintained by such critics as Ken Burns that they "were far weaker" without offering any qualifications on their opinions, would benefit greatly from taking a second look at the Reds' performance in game two.

When Federal Judge Kenesaw Mountain Landis was asked for a comment on the first two games of the series he replied, "The Reds are the most formidable machine I've ever seen in my many years as a fan. Individually and collectively the team is wonderful. I have learned through years of experience on the bench to maintain a judicial attitude and I promise to do this provided the Reds do not keep on making this such a lopsided affair."[4] Judge Landis then left for Chicago to see the games that were about to begin there.

Perhaps knowing that Judge Landis was such a staunch White Sox fan might help explain his downright bitterness in deciding to hand out lifetime bans to eight White Sox players in this series two years later when he became the first commissioner of baseball, despite only circumstantial evidence of a conspiracy to throw the series.

However, for fans (and any players too) that might have been gambling on the series, the opportunity to hedge their bets was now being offered as the Reds, following their win in game two, were placed at 9-5 favorites to win the series.

As for those so called "Famous Fifty" from Philadelphia, at the conclusion of the game they returned by bus to their headquarters at the Grand Hotel then had dinner. Following dinner they all headed for the Keith's Theatre and took in a first-class vaudeville show, then hurried over to the Big Four Railroad Station and boarded special Pullmans for the overnight trip north to Chicago for game three.

Box Score Game Two

Chicago	ab	r	h	rbi	Cincinnati	ab	r	h	rbi
J. Collins, rf	4	0	0	0	Rath, 2b	3	1	0	0
E. Collins, 2b	3	0	0	0	Daubert, 1b	3	0	0	0
Weaver, 3b	4	0	2	0	Groh, 3b	2	1	0	0
Jackson, lf	4	0	3	0	Roush, cf	2	1	1	1
Felsch, cf	2	0	0	0	Duncan, lf	1	1	0	0
Gandil, 1b	4	0	1	0	Kopf, ss	3	0	1	2

Chicago	ab	r	h	rbi	Cincinnati	ab	r	h	rbi
Risberg, ss	4	1	1	0	Neale, rf	3	0	1	1
Schalk, c	4	1	2	0	Rariden, c	3	0	1	0
Williams, p	3	0	1	0	Sallee, p	3	0	0	0
McMullin, ph	1	0	0	0					

Chicago	ip	h	r	er	bb	so
Williams	8	4	4	4	6	1

Cincinnati	ip	h	r	er	bb	so
Sallee	9	10	2	0	1	2

LOB Chicago 7, Cincinnati 3, E Risberg 1, Daubert 1, Neale 1, 2b Jackson, Weaver, 3b Kopf, S Felsch 2, Daubert, Duncan, SB Gandil

•Two runs scored on Neale's throwing error in the seventh.

CHAPTER FOUR

Game Three

At Chicago, October 3, 1919

	1	2	3	4	5	6	7	8	9	R	H	E
Cincinnati	0	0	0	0	0	0	0	0	0	0	3	1
Chicago	0	2	0	1	0	0	0	0		3	7	0

Fisher, Luque (8)
Kerr

Following game two in Cincinnati both the Reds and White Sox, along with a contingency of their respective fans and various sportswriters, boarded night trains and traveled over the Big Four Tracks north to Chicago. After the Reds arrived at Union Station in the morning they checked into the Congress Hotel on Michigan Avenue.

The first two games of the series played in Cincinnati had been a huge success at that gate with a total attendance of 60,201 and total receipts of $195,914. Therefore, it was anticipated that the fever-pitched fan interest in the series would continue in Chicago. However, when the gates to Comiskey Park were opened there were plenty of empty seats in the bleachers. The attendance for the first game was 29,126, the smallest gate so far in the three games played.

It was widely expected that Reds manager Pat Moran, leading the series 2-0 and having four rested starting pitchers available for service in game three, would give the ball to Hod Eller. However, he surprised most observers when he selected eight-year veteran Ray Fisher for the task at hand. Fisher had spent his entire career with the New York High-landers/Yankees before spending the 1918 season in the U.S. Army. On March 15, 1919, he was acquired by the Reds on waivers and had a 14-5 record for the Reds in the 1919 season.

Eddie Cicotte had wanted to start game three for the White Sox with only one day's rest. Kid Gleason had actually considered using his ace thus giving all the chance to see that Cicotte was still a great pitcher. However, Gleason also surprised everyone when he selected Dickie Kerr to pitch game three.

Pint-sized Dickie Kerr, 5'7" and 155 pounds soaking wet, was a left hander from Paris, Texas. For some unknown reason Kerr was inaccurately portrayed in the movie *Eight Men Out* as a right hander. Perhaps the producers could not find an actor who was a southpaw.

However, Dickie Kerr was a most unlikely choice by Kid Gleason for the task of taming the rampaging Reds. He had been rejected by several major league teams including Cleveland and was declared too small for the big leagues by the St. Louis Browns. In 1918 he had been signed by Branch Rickey (president and manager) for the St. Louis Cardinals. However, Rickey never brought him up to the parent club and eventually placed Kerr on waivers. Kerr cleared waivers through every National League team and wound up pitching in the American Association for Milwaukee. Charles Comiskey then signed him for the White Sox in the 1919 season and Kerr started 17 games and had a very respectable record of 13-7 with an ERA of 2.88.

It was a beautiful day for a World Series game in Chicago. Even though there was not a full house in Comiskey Park, the White Sox fans were determined to show their heroes that they were behind them regardless of the 2-0 deficit in the series. The allegiance of the fans obviously had an effect on the Sox players from the start of the game as Dickie Kerr walked toward the mound and umpire Quigley took his position behind the plate.

From the start Kerr handcuffed the Reds' batters with a sharp break-ing curve ball. In the first inning he set down the first three hitters in order, getting Rath to ground out, Risberg to Gandil, Daubert to fly out to Felsch and fanning Heinie Groh.

In the bottom half of the first inning Ray Fisher looked effective also as he set the Sox down in order. Nemo Leibold, making his first appear-ance in the series, lined out to Neale who made a shoestring catch. Eddie Collins hit a weak ball back to the mound, Fisher to Daubert, and Buck Weaver lifted a fly ball that was caught by Daubert.

In the second inning Edd Roush led off against Kerr and grounded out. Next Pat Duncan lifted a soft fly back of second for a hit. Larry Kopf, attempting a hit-and-run, grounded the ball to Risberg, who lost control of it just long enough to lose a double play, but recovered and threw Kopf out at first. Kerr then got Greasy Neale to ground out, Collins to Gandil.

In the bottom of the second Shoeless Joe Jackson led off and gave the home-team crowd something to shout about when he ripped into Ray Fisher's first pitch and drove a clean single to left. Happy Felsch then laid down a bunt toward the mound. The bunt was not a very good one and most probably Felsch had topped a Fisher spitball, which in 1919 was still legal. Nonetheless, Fisher in a haste to make a force play at second threw the ball into center, probably grabbing the wet spot on the ball. Joe Jackson fell down rounding second, but recovered in time to reach third in front of a perfect throw by Roush to Groh. Felsch took second on the play.

Reds manager Pat Moran decided to pull the infield in to cut off a potential run. Chick Gandil came up to bat and hit the first pitch from Fisher for a single between Daubert and Rath. The hit scored both Jackson and Felsch. When Neale attempted to cut down Felsch at the plate, Gandil raced for second. For the first time in 20 innings in the series the White Sox had the lead in a game.

Next up was Swede Risberg who made two attempts at a sacrifice, then began to hit away until he was grazed on the leg by one of Fisher's pitches. With Risberg on first and Gandil on second, Ray Schalk attempted to sacrifice. What follows is one of the most interesting and controversial plays of the 1919 World Series.

Schalk laid down a bunt between Fisher and Groh that looked safe, however, Chick Gandil was forced at third on a late throw by Fisher. There was some immediate speculation that Gandil had intentionally loafed on the play.

Sportswriter Hugh S. Fullerton reported the play as follows: "The Reds were caught flat-footed and the ball rolled toward third. Gandil, coming up from second, had the play beaten by a block, but he stood up and seemed to be conversing with Kid Gleason (coaching at third base), when Fisher suddenly grabbed the ball and flashed it to Groh. Gandil made a fox-trot step to touch third, but was forced out on a clean base hit."[1]

However, sportswriter Ren Mulford, Jr., who viewed the same play as Fullerton, made no allegation of Gandil loafing on the play. He simply wrote, "Schalk tried to sacrifice. Fisher gathered the ball and just did nip Gandil at third. The play was immediately duplicated when Kerr's rap to Fisher led to Risberg's undoing at third."[2]

Tom Swope of the *Cincinnati Post*, Johnny Evers of the *United Press* and Jim Nasium of the *Philadelphia Inquirer* are a few of the many sports-writers following game three that never mentioned the Gandil play in their columns.

So there are conflicting views on the intensity and intention of Gandil's base running in the bottom of the second. There is no film or videotape to confirm the worst or the best in his effort. Consequently legend suggesting that Gandil wanted to be thrown out and thereby impede the White Sox rally that he had begun has taken precedence in the matter over the ensuing eight-plus decades. Even if Chick Gandil was attempting to throw games in the series, it is also possible that he was simply confused by the play and hesitated going to third.

Nonetheless, Fisher brought the curtain down on the bottom of the second when Dickie Kerr hit a grounder back to the box that Fisher fielded and tossed to Groh at third forcing Risberg.

In the top of the third Bill Rariden led off and grounded out to Weaver. Ray Fisher, a decent hitter for a pitcher who had a season batting average of .271, was next up. He hit the ball weakly down the third-base line. Kerr raced over and fell upon the ball as it was about to go foul, allowing Fisher to reach first with a hit. However, Kerr put the lid on any possible Reds rally by getting Rath to pop out to Risberg and Daubert to force Fisher at second.

In the bottom of the third it looked like the White Sox were going to score a few more runs when Eddie Collins and Buck Weaver led off with singles. The loyal Comiskey crowd then went wild with anticipation as Joe Jackson came up to bat. However, he pushed a little fly over the head of Fisher that the slick-fielding Jake Daubert raced over and caught. After making the play Daubert failed to notice that Morrie Rath was standing on first waiting to double up Weaver. However, the Reds got their double play anyway to end the inning when Felsch hit the ball hard to Rath, who turned the ball into a double play.

Heinie Groh walked to open the fourth inning. However, the Reds could do nothing with the base runner as Kerr continued to dominate them. Edd Roush followed with a slow grounder to Risberg who made a quick throw to first retiring him. Groh took second on the play but was doubled up when Pat Duncan lined the ball to Risberg who pegged the ball to Collins covering second.

Chick Gandil opened the Sox half of the fourth grounding out, Groh to Daubert. Swede Risberg then leaned in to one of Fisher's pitches and tripled to right, the ball bounding past Neale. With Ray Schalk coming to bat, Kid Gleason called for a squeeze play. Schalk hit a sharp tap that caromed away from Fisher, as he slipped for safety. Risberg dashed home from third with the White Sox third run of the game and their first earned run of the series after 21⅔ innings. When Schalk then attempted to steal second Rariden threw him out.

In the top of the fifth inning Larry Kopf led off with the Reds third and final hit of the game off Kerr, a line shot to right. Greasy Neale then forced Kopf, Gandil to Risberg. Bill Rariden then grounded out and so did Ray Fisher to end the inning.

Fisher retired the White Sox in order in the bottom of the fifth.

In the top of the sixth Kerr retired the Reds in order.

In the bottom half of the sixth a duel ensued between Fisher and Joe Jackson. On Fisher's first pitch Jackson swung so hard he fell down. The crowd was highly amused. Next, Fisher uncorked a pitch that flew several feet over Jackson's head. The next pitch was a slow ball outside. Jackson then fouled the next pitch right into Rariden's mitt, but he could not handle it. Jackson then hit a Texas leaguer just out of the reach of Larry Kopf. However, on the next pitch Jackson attempted to steal second and was thrown out when Kopf made a great stop of Rariden's low throw. Fisher continued his wildness by walking Happy Felsch after having him down no balls and two strikes. Felsch was then thrown out attempting to steal second base, Rariden to Rath. Fisher then fanned Gandil to end the inning.

In the top of the seventh Dickie Kerr, having great control and a superb curve ball, set the Reds down in order again. Kerr had now retired nine Reds batters in a row.

In the bottom of the inning Swede Risberg led off and hit a grounder towards short. Heinie Groh raced over in front of Kopf, speared the ball and threw to Daubert at first for the out. The Chicago fans gave Groh a huge applause for his effort. Fisher then got Schalk and Kerr to ground out to end the inning.

In the top of the eighth inning Kerr struck out Neale and got Rariden to ground out, Collins to Gandil. Pat Moran then came to the conclusion that Fisher had seen enough action for the day and sent Sherwood (Sherry) Magee up to pinch-hit for him. Magee was a veteran ball player who had played for the Phillies 1904–14, then was traded to the Braves. In 1919 he was finishing up his brilliant career playing with the Reds. Magee had 2,169 career hits and was the National League batting champion in 1910 with a .331 average. Kerr quickly disposed of Magee getting him to fly out to Leibold, thereby retiring the last 12 batters in a row he had faced.

In the bottom of the eighth Adolfo Luque was sent in to pitch for the Reds. Luque was a novelty for his time. A native of Cuba, he was referred to as the "The Pride of Havana." In 1919 the Reds used him primarily in relief. But in 1923 he would lead the National League in wins (27-8) and

winning percentage (.771). The first batter to face Luque was Nemo Leibold and he promptly struck out.

Although the Reds were heading down to their first defeat in the series,
they had been riding the White Sox unmercifully all day. Earlier in the game
Eddie Collins had wanted to fight Reds reserve infielder Jimmy Smith who
had been riding him from the bench. During the game Smith had wanted
to fight with Happy Felsch too, until the umpires intervened. When Nemo
Leibold struck out against Luque, Heinie Groh gave him a severe tongue
lashing from third. Leibold could not handle it and all at once came charging down the third-base line, bat in hand toward Groh. Kid Gleason coaching at third had to wave Leibold away.

Luque ended the inning by getting Eddie Collins to ground out, then
getting Buck Weaver to do likewise.

Dickie Kerr appeared just as dominating in the ninth inning as he did
in the first. He quickly disposed of the Reds by getting Rath to ground out,
striking out Jake Daubert and then getting Groh to ground out, Weaver
to Gandil, to end the game. Kerr had retired the last 15 batters in the game
to face him.

With a superb curve ball and control Dickie Kerr gave up just three
hits and the Reds never got a man past second base. He struck out four
and walked only one in pitching the first shutout of the series. With a little luck Kerr could have pitched a no-hitter. He himself stopped Ray
Fisher's slow roller in the third that would have gone foul had he not
touched it. In the second Pat Duncan lifted a little fly that fell safe back of
second. Had Eddie Collins been playing a little farther towards first in the
fifth, he may have stopped Larry Kopf's leadoff single.

Nonetheless, Ray Fisher should get credit for pitching pretty decent
during game two. He gave up just three runs on seven hits. Fisher walked
only two batters and fanned one. In fact Fisher may have actually thrown
the game away with a wild throw into center on Ray Schalk's squeeze bunt
in the second inning that eventually led to two Chicago runs.

Other than the miscue by Fisher, the Reds' defense was brilliant with
Heinie Groh and Jake Daubert making great stops all day and catcher Bill
Rariden throwing out runners at second. However, it is prudent to point
out that the Reds were the superior team in fielding in 1919, having a season fielding average of .974 as opposed to the White Sox's average of .969.

Popular belief has maintained that sportswriter Hugh S. Fullerton
along with Christy Mathewson thought something smelled about the 1919
World Series and the two were supposed to be sitting in the press box
pointing out plays that they felt were suspect. However, other than com-
ments about Chick Gandil's base running in the second inning, Fullerton

had nothing negative to say about the Sox in his column following game three.

What is so unfortunate about the Hollywood version of Fullerton and Mathewson becoming self-appointed watch dogs of the series is that the producers of the film *Eight Men Out* decided to eliminate Mathewson's part and instead create a part for author Studs Terkel to play as Fullerton's buddy scrutinizing the plays in the series. The producers Barbara Boyle and Jerry Offsay really missed a golden opportunity here to chronicle an ailing Christy Mathewson suffering from the effects of mustard gas from his participation in World War I and at the same time agonizing over the legitimacy of certain plays in the series. But this was not the only historical accuracy compromised in the film. It had many from beginning to the end.

However, in all fairness to the producers of *Eight Men Out*, everyone who writes or produces something in regard to the 1919 World Series, from news articles to books to films to Internet reports, appears to believe that they have license to distort the facts and present them in any way that seems to assist their point. Due to the controversy surrounding the 1919 World Series, there is no objectivity and it has been open season on the facts of the event since the last pitch on October 9, 1919.

When it came to the Reds fielding in game three, Fullerton had nothing but heaps of praise. The Reds seemed to read Kid Gleason's hit-and-run attempts perfectly. Fullerton took notice of this fact and wrote following game three, "Moran very obviously outguessed the Sox in the battle of wits. The White Sox hit and run went sadly awry. Whether it was Moran or Bill Rariden is a question, but whenever the White Sox attempted play, the ball was hurried wide and the runner chopped down at second."[3]

Fullerton was also particularly high in the praise of the fielding demonstrated by Reds Captain Heinie Groh. "Groh's defensive work was one of the most brilliant and desperate ever seen since that of Herzog in the famous Giant-Red Sox struggle [a reference to the 1912 World Series won by Boston four games to three, where Giant third baseman Buck Herzog handled sixteen attempts without an error]. Groh broke down two drives today that would have smeared runs all over the score board. He smashed up two tallies and was the entire defense in the critical moments."[4]

Regardless of the loss in game three the Reds' confidence was unwavering that they had the White Sox beat in the series. All through the game the Reds verbally abused the White Sox at will. Tom Swope in his column mentioned, "all the Reds chattered away at the White Sox like a bunch of monkeys, telling them how punk they were as a ball club and reminding them they have had to be given all the runs they have made so far in the series."[5]

This was obviously a reference to the fact that White Sox did not score their earned run until the second inning of the third game and then scored most of their runs in the game as a result of Reds miscues.

The Reds' taunting of the mighty White Sox even continued after the game. As the players were leaving the field using the same tunnel in Comiskey Park to get to their clubhouses, Jimmy Smith caught up with Eddie Collins who had spit at him late in the game. Smith had avoided the spit, but was still very angry. Collins attempted to stick out his hand to Smith, but Jimmy hastened that if he had the opportunity tomorrow, he would spit in Collins' eye.

The Reds' confidence as a ball club, demonstrated by this open display of razing towards the White Sox, further contradicts the folklore that has taken hold over the years since the series that they felt vastly inferior to the White Sox. Geoffrey Ward and Ken Burns in the PBS series *Baseball* had the unmitigated gall to refer to the 1919 National League Champion Reds as a "better paid, but weaker team."

However, the most outrageous unsubstantiated remark in regards to this inferiority complex attributed to the Reds appears in a book *Greatest Moments in Baseball* by George L. Flynn, published in 1987. Flynn takes liberty with historical accuracy to assert that Edd Roush was to have said prior to game one, "Compared to the White Sox, we are just an ordinary team." Roush, the 1919 National League batting champion, was a very fierce competitor and would have never made such a comment. In fact had Roush made such a comment, his teammates, including brawlers Jimmy Smith and Sherry Magee, would have severely taken him to task for it. Roush, who openly fought with John McGraw when a member of the New York Giants, hit over .300 in 11 straight seasons and was elected to the Baseball Hall of Fame in 1962. He maintained to all who raised the issue before him until his dying day on March 21, 1988, that the 1919 Reds were a superior team to the White Sox.

But good fielding, bad base running, conspiracy suspicions, inferiority complexes and all the like aside, the day in game three belonged to White Sox Dickie Kerr, a cast-off, a guy too small to play big league ball.

The *Philadelphia Inquirer* stated that "Kerr seemed to grow taller in each inning."

Tom Swope, Sporting Editor of the *Cincinnati Post,* wrote, "It was a real treat to see the way the Reds battled the Sox late in the game when it was evident to everyone in the park that Dick Kerr had something on the ball that made him almost unhittable."[6]

Box Score Game Three

Cincinnati	ab	r	h	rbi	Chicago	ab	r	h	rbi
Rath, 2b	4	0	0	0	Leibold, rf	4	0	0	0
Daubert, 1b	4	0	0	0	E. Collins, 2b	4	0	1	0
Groh, 3b	4	0	0	0	Weaver, 3b	4	0	1	0
Roush, cf	3	0	0	0	Jackson, lf	3	1	2	0
Duncan, lf	3	0	1	0	Felsch, cf	2	1	0	0
Kopf, ss	3	0	1	0	Gandil, 1b	3	0	1	2
Neale, cf	3	0	0	0	Risberg, ss	2	1	1	0
Rariden, c	3	0	0	0	Schalk, c	3	0	1	1
Fisher, p	2	0	1	0	Kerr, p	3	0	0	0
Magee, ph	1	0	0	0					
Luque, p	0	0	0	0					

Cincinnati	ip	h	r	er	bb	so
Fisher	7	7	3	1	2	1
Luque	1	0	0	0	0	1

Chicago						
Kerr	9	3	0	0	1	4

LOB Cincinnati 3, Chicago 2, E Fisher 1, 3b Risberg

CHAPTER FIVE

Game Four

At Chicago, October 4, 1919

	1	2	3	4	5	6	7	8	9	R	H	E
Cincinnati	0	0	0	0	2	0	0	0	0	2	5	2
Chicago	0	0	0	0	0	0	0	0	0	0	3	2

Ring
Cicotte

Total attendance for the first three games of the series was 89,327. Now that number was about to swell with the 34,363 in attendance at Comiskey Park for game four, the largest gate of the series.

Jimmy Ring was selected by Pat Moran to start for the Reds against Eddie Cicotte for the White Sox. Ring, who had a season record of 10-9 for the Reds in 1919, was a hard throwing right hander who had a tendency for wildness. However, in the 1919 World Series, Ring would post the best ERA (0.64) of all the pitchers.

There had been some speculation that Moran would start Hod Eller, a 20-game winner in the 1919 season. Some of the sportswriters though had the opinion that Eller did not pitch well in front of hostile crowds. But that is probably more myth than fact because Hod Eller pitched some excellent games on the road against the New York Giants in 1919 coming down the stretch run for the pennant.

Prior to game four Tom Swope wrote in the *Cincinnati Post*:

> The Sox now know the Reds are not only a real ball club but one that doesn't respect the alleged superiority the Sox used to feel was theirs. Not only does the series now stand two games to one in favor of the Reds, in spite of yesterday's defeat, but the outlook for the next two games is in Cincinnati's favor.
>
> Pat's boys still believe in themselves as much as they ever did and they have two great pitchers ready to shoot at the Sox in Eller and Ring, neither whom has worked so far in the series. And then there are Walt Ruether and Slim Sallee who can pitch in turn starting any day Pat elects to bring them back to the hill.
>
> To combat this quartet Kid Gleason again must depend on Cicotte and Williams, his beaten stars, or take a chance on second string material which he is not likely to do. The Sox are feigning a feeling of confidence and bragging that yesterday's game is proof they are about to land on the Reds with both feet and sweep the world championship dreams out of the Reds domes. But they can't be half as sure of this as they would like to believe they are. The picture of what happened to Cicotte and Williams at Cincinnati is bound to lessen their confidence in themselves.[1]

True, Chicago did indeed have a pitching deficit in the World Series regardless of what Cicotte and Williams may or may not have been up to. One fact that is continuously overlooked in regards to the White Sox pitching staff in the 1919 World Series is that Urban "Red" Faber, the White Sox hero of the 1917 World Series win over the New York Giants, was sitting out the series against the Reds with a sore arm and supposedly the flu too! Faber, who had won three games in the 1917 World Series, would recover from his ailments and go on to win 20 or more games for the White Sox in 1920 (23), 1921 (25) and 1922 (21).

Taking Faber out of the White Sox pitching rotation for the entire series put added stress on Cicotte and Williams to win, and Kid Gleason was not going to be able to just pull a Dickie Kerr out of a hat every third day.

Therefore, Eddie Cicotte was about to start game four on just two days rest following his defeat in game one.

In regards to the Reds' chances in game four, Reds captain Heinie Groh had this bit of optimism, "Cicotte is the bird we like to hit."[2]

Cicotte completed his warm-up pitches; Morrie Rath led off for the Reds and drove a clean single over Buck Weaver's head. However, Cicotte quickly ended the inning as Jake Daubert hit into a double play and Heinie Groh hit a little pop fly that Swede Risberg went back and put away.

Jimmy Ring then quickly set the Sox down in order in the first on a little fly ball by Leibold caught by Daubert, a pop fly by Eddie Collins hauled in by Rath and a line shot by Weaver into the hands of Greasy Neale.

Cicotte followed by setting the Reds down in order with ease in the second.

In the bottom of the second Joe Jackson led off against Ring by hitting the ball into short center and then hustling to take two bases on the hit. Hap Felsch then laid down a sacrifice, Ring to Rath, and Jackson took third. Chick Gandil followed by hitting a fly ball within a yard of the plate that Groh caught. Ring walked Risberg. Risberg then stole second when catcher Ivy Wingo stopped a wild pitch from Ring. Ring then threw four consecutive balls walking Schalk to load the bases. Eddie Cicotte then came up to bat amongst a cheering Comiskey Park crowd. However, Ring got out of the inning unscathed when Cicotte hit the ball to Rath who made a running stop and threw him out at first.

Greasy Neale led off for the Reds in the third and grounded out. After Ivy Wingo got the Reds' second hit off Cicotte by singling to center, Cicotte struck out Ring, and then when Wingo attempted to steal second base he was thrown out by Ray Schalk.

In the Sox half of the third, Nemo Leibold led off by lining out to Neale. Ring then plucked Eddie Collins in the ribs with a curve. Buck Weaver grounded out to Daubert and Collins took second on the play. Joe Jackson then got on base when Rath fumbled his grounder. Collins took third on the play. However, Happy Felsch ended the inning when he hit Ring's first pitch to Heinie Groh who threw to first for the out.

Cicotte once again set down the Reds in order in the fourth.

The pitching duel between Ring and Cicotte continued as Ring set the Sox down in order in the bottom of the fourth.

Edd Roush was retired to lead off the top of the fifth, Schalk to Gandil.

Then the infamous, controversial and well-chronicled fifth inning events unfolded when Pat Duncan hit the ball back hard at Cicotte. Cicotte fumbled the ball, then recovered and threw wild to first, Duncan taking second on the error. Larry Kopf followed by hitting a line-drive single to left and Duncan took third. Joe Jackson's fast fielding kept Kopf's hit from going through for two or even three bases. Jackson then made a throw toward the plate and all at once, Cicotte stuck his hands up and deflected the ball out of the reach of Schalk waiting at the plate. The ball rolled away to the stands with Schalk in hot pursuit while Cicotte ran around in circles, not knowing exactly what to do as the speedy Duncan scored and Kopf went to second.

Greasy Neale then hit a curve from Cicotte squarely and the ball went over Jackson's head in left field for a double. Kopf scored on the hit. Ivy Wingo then hit a hard grounder to Eddie Collins who threw him out at first, Neale taking third. However, Cicotte finally got out of trouble when Jimmy Ring hit a hot grounder to Eddie Collins, who threw him out to end the inning.

White Sox bat boy, thirteen-year-old Clyde Winn, said that when Cicotte came back to the dugout following the fifth he was foaming at the mouth. "He was cussin to beat the band when he came to the dugout after the fifth inning. The Reds got the breaks, thassal; they coulda win this game with a pair of dice. Thassal."[3]

The top of the fifth inning is regarded as the most suspect of all innings in the 1919 World Series by those who have analyzed the conspiracy theory. Both Cincinnati runs were scored as result of errors by Eddie Cicotte. Cicotte's wild toss to first following Duncan's smash back to the box and his deflection of Joe Jackson's perfect throw from left field to attempt to get Duncan at the plate caused many to believe that the rumors of a fix were true.

Jimmy Ring continued to stifle the White Sox in the bottom of the fifth. Eddie Cicotte grounded out, Daubert to Ring. Then Nemo Leibold grounded to Groh, who made a wild throw to first. Leibold went to second. Eddie Collins hit a smash to Groh who threw to Rath for the out. With Leibold holding on second, Buck Weaver hit an easy one-hopper to Jake Daubert to end the inning.

Cicotte set the Reds down in order in the top of the sixth.

Joe Jackson led off the Sox half of the inning and grounded out, Kopf to Daubert. Happy Felsch then unloaded a long drive to left only a few feet from the bleachers. Pat Duncan went back and made a great catch.

The fans at Comiskey Park had a habit, when the wind was compatible, of tearing up paper and letting it drift out to left field. This habit was particularly irritating to Pat Duncan, but fortunately when he made the great catch on Felsch's blast no paper was in the air.

Chick Gandil then smashed a single through the box. This was the second hit in the game by the Sox off Ring. However, Gandil died at second when Ring got Risberg to hit a long fly foul down the right field line that Neale ran over and caught falling into the seats.

In the top of the seventh Cicotte once again set the Reds down in order. Cicotte had now retired the last eight Reds batters in order.

Despite six shutout innings Ring was still showing signs of wildness and with his third pitch he plunked Ray Schalk in the back. This was Ring's second hit batter in the game. However, he then settled down and retired Cicotte, Leibold and Eddie Collins in order ending the inning.

In the top of the eighth Eddie Cicotte got Greasy Neale on a bouncer back to the box. Ivy Wingo followed with his second hit of the game, a single into center. As Jimmy Ring came up to bat the partisan White Sox crowd gave him a nice ovation. Ring then hit into a double play, Cicotte to Risberg to Gandil.

In the Sox half of the eighth, Buck Weaver hit a fly to right that was about to fall safe between Daubert and Neale when Morrie Rath raced in between them and made a great catch. Ring then struck out Joe Jackson on a fastball. However, Happy Felsch, in the hole against Ring with no balls and two strikes, then singled over third base. Chick Gandil was then caught looking at a third strike to end the inning.

Cicotte set the Reds down in order in the ninth.

Swede Risberg was the first Sox batter in the bottom of the ninth and grounded out, Ring to Daubert. Kid Gleason then pinch-hit for Cicotte, sending Eddie Murphy up to hit for him. Eddie Murphy was a journeyman reserve outfielder who had been a regular for Connie Mack's pennant winning Philadelphia A's in 1913 and 1914. Charles Comiskey purchased him from the A's for $13,500 on July 15, 1915.

Ring got Murphy to fly out to Roush. Nemo Leibold then followed with a hard liner down to third that Heinie Groh threw himself in front of ending the game.

Jimmy Ring, despite hitting two batters and walking three, went the distance allowing just three hits and striking out two batters in pitching the second shutout of the series. In fact Ring only threw one less pitch for strikes (32) than did Cicotte (33) in the game.

Eddie Cicotte pitched a fair game as well, giving up just five hits and two runs. All things considered, it was not Eddie's day. Nonalleged conspirators Nemo Leibold, Eddie Collins and Ray Schalk continued to waive anemic bats and overall the White Sox left ten men on base in the game. Also Cicotte himself failed to deliver a hit off Ring in the bottom of the second with the bases loaded and two out.

But without question it was Eddie Cicotte's shabby fielding and two errors that made the difference in the game. He recovered in the sixth inning from the disaster of the fifth, but the damage was done and Jimmy Ring just got stronger every inning until the end, literally handcuffing the White Sox batters.

Tom Swope of the *Cincinnati Post* rationalized Cicotte's attempt in the fifth inning to field Pat Duncan's hot smash towards him as "trying hard to redeem himself for his one-sided defeat in the first series game and leaped for the ball. A taller man than Cicotte probably would have got the ball and a wiser one would have let it go for the shortstop to handle."[4]

Sherry Magee, Edd Roush, Earle "Greasy" Neale (left to right), Cincinnati Reds, 1919. (*The Sporting News.*)

"Cicotte was rattled to start with and this rattled him more. Instead of allowing Buck Weaver to try for the play, he ran and picked up the ball and then heaved to the grandstand allowing Duncan to reach second."

Next Larry Kopf singled sending Duncan to third, and when Cicotte cut off Joe Jackson's throw from left, Duncan scored.

However, Heinie Groh pointed out that even if Cicotte had held the much ballyhooed throw from Jackson keeping Duncan at third, then he would have still scored on Greasy Neale's double that followed and most probably Kopf would have too.

Nonetheless most conspiracy theorists have totally ignored for the past 81 years the critical fact that Eddie Cicotte, despite his brilliance as a hurler, was simply no Grover Cleveland Alexander when it came to fielding on the mound. Cicotte had a notorious record as a very poor fielding pitcher. Of all the starting pitchers in the 1919 World Series, Cicotte had the poorest lifetime fielding average. Furthermore only one other pitcher in the series, reliever Grover Loudermilk, had a poorer lifetime fielding record than Cicotte. He was so poor that on occasions the Sox fans referred to him as Grover Buttermilk.

Listed below are the lifetime fielding averages for the starting pitchers in the series.

Name	Years	Errors	Fielding Ave.
Hod Eller	5	4	.980
Slim Sallee	11	32	.973
Dutch Ruether	11	32	.972
Jimmy Ring	12	25	.967
Claude Williams	7	12	.955
Dickie Kerr	4	13	.953
Ray Fisher	10	39	.946
Eddie Cicotte	14	70	.942

With the Reds out in front in the series with a surprising 3-1 advantage, alibis for the White Sox's poor performance were being manufactured in high gear by those, chiefly the press, who thought the Sox were invincible in the series. The alibi most often heard was that the White Sox were just not hitting. In fact the pale hose crew were hitting a pale .211 after the fourth game of the series. While Joe Jackson was hitting an even .400, it was all downhill in the Sox batting average department from there.

Eddie Collins, supposedly the greatest second baseman in the game who is at his best with something on the line and had hit .319 during the regular season, was hitting .143 in the series. Nemo Leibold, a .302 hitter, so far had not gotten a hit in the series and was 0 for 9. Buck Weaver, who had hit .296 in the 1919 regular season, was hitting a mediocre .250.

The reality was that the Reds weren't doing much better with the stick, hitting just .234. The Reds' two best hitters, Heinie Groh and Edd Roush, were having a miserable series so far. Groh, a .310 hitter during the regular season, and Edd Roush, the National League batting champion, both were batting just .091 after the first four games.

Both teams so far had 26 hits. But the difference in the win column was a factor of the Reds getting hits that counted.

Sportswriter Ross Tenney summarized the White Sox's woes in the series so far this way. "The White Sox in this series have been hit by the biggest batting slump that they have experienced all season. When their pitchers wabbled during the regular season they went in and batted out victories by the might of their swatting. But so far they have looked like the weakest team at bat that ever entered a World Series."[5]

Box Score Game Four

Cincinnati	ab	r	h	rbi	Chicago	ab	r	h	rbi
Rath, 2b	4	0	1	0	Leibold, rf	5	0	0	0
Daubert, 1b	4	0	0	0	E. Collins, 2b	3	0	0	0
Groh, 3b	4	0	0	0	Weaver, 3b	4	0	0	0
Roush, cf	3	0	0	0	Jackson, lf	4	0	1	0
Duncan, lf	3	1	0	0	Felsch, cf	3	0	1	0
Kopf, ss	3	1	1	1	Gandil, 1b	4	0	1	0
Neale, cf	3	0	1	1	Risberg, ss	3	0	0	0
Wingo, c	3	0	2	0	Schalk, c	1	0	0	0
Ring, p	3	0	0	0	Cicotte, p	3	0	0	0
					Murphy, ph	1	0	0	0

Cincinnati	ip	h	r	er	bb	so
Ring	9	3	0	0	3	2

Chicago						
Cicotte	9	5	2	0	0	2

LOB Cincinnati 1, Chicago 10, E Cicotte 2, Groh, 2b Jackson, Neale, S Felsch, SB Risberg, HBP Ring 2

CHAPTER SIX

Game Five

At Chicago, October 5, 1919

	1	2	3	4	5	6	7	8	9	R	H	E
Cincinnati			GAME POSTPONED — RAIN									
Chicago												

At Chicago, October 6, 1919

	1	2	3	4	5	6	7	8	9	R	H	E
Cincinnati	0	0	0	0	0	4	0	0	1	5	4	0
Chicago	0	0	0	0	0	0	0	0	0	0	3	3

Eller
Williams, Mayer (9)

Following game four an all-night rainstorm swept through Chicago into the morning hours leaving the playing field at Comiskey Park too wet to permit game five to be played. In various places the ballpark was even flooded.

As the rain subsided in the late morning there was hope that the game might still be played, but at 11:00 A.M. Umpires Rigler and Evans made a visit to Comiskey Park and issued the official announcement that the game would not be played.

Despite the Reds now having a 3-1 edge in the series, all through the morning trains brought legions of fans into town from nearby points in hopes that the weather would clear and the game would be played. Thousands were at Comiskey Park. The fans were disappointed that it was raining, but even more disappointed as they received the official announcement that the game was postponed and they had to head back for home.

The delay in the series gave the odds makers a lot of opportunity to rework the numbers for the favorites, and the morning line now had the Reds as 4-1 favorites to win the series. But interestingly enough the odds for game five with Hod Eller slated to pitch against Lefty Williams had the Reds only a 10-9 favorite to win game five.

The rain delay gave the players on both teams the chance to rest and gave the fans and sportswriters an opportunity to rehash the first four games of the series. So in various hotels in downtown Chicago — the Auditorium, Blackstone, Congress, LaSalle and Sherman House — between the card games and crap shooting, philosophers and statisticians offered their take on where the series had been so far and where it was heading. This would have been an ample opportunity for anyone convinced that the series was not being played on the up and up to raise the question either publicly or in the press. It was just a few days ago that the White Sox's superiority was supposed to have been unstoppable by the Reds in the series. Regardless of the Reds' acknowledged edge in pitching, it was the prediction of the experts that the Reds pitchers would be duck soup for the White Sox hitters who had led the American League during the 1919 season with a team batting average of .287. Surprisingly, during this intermission in the series the issue of a fix or conspiracy never came up publicly and there was nothing written about a possible fix in newspapers throughout the country.

It was pretty evident to everyone that the White Sox had been outclassed by the Reds so far in the series. In the first four games the White Sox had left 25 men on base. They had a total of 37 men get to first base, 26 on hits, 7 on walks, 2 by being hit by a pitched ball and 2 as a result of errors. Yet despite having put 37 runners on base in the first four games, the Sox had scored just one earned run as a result of their hitting efforts. The one earned run that they had scored came as a result of a ball that took a bad bounce away from Greasy Neale when Swede Risberg hit a liner to right in the bottom of the fourth inning in the third game.

In contrast, during the first four games the Reds had gotten only 25 hits, had nine men reach first as a result of walks and despite being shutout by Dickie Kerr in the third game had still scored 12 earned runs.

But the biggest difference in the Reds' margin of victories over the first four games was their ability to score runs when the opportunities were present as opposed to the White Sox who could not push runners across the plate when they had the chance. In fact the White Sox had only scored six runs in the first four games and two of those runs came as a result of Ray Fisher's wild throw into center field in the third game.

Of course the spectacular fielding of Heinie Groh, Morrie Rath and Edd Roush was paramount in stopping Sox rallies dead-cold time and time again. In the second inning of the fourth game the White Sox had the bases full when Eddie Cicotte hit a hard grounder that Rath made a spectacular stop on and then threw to first ending the inning and quashing the Sox hopes. In the eighth inning Rath again made a spectacular catch of a fly ball that prevented a two-base hit and a White Sox run. Groh time and time again made diving catches that snuffed out Sox rallies. In game one Roush made great running catches of long hits by Buck Weaver and Shano Collins and then in game two Roush may have preserved the Reds 4-2 victory when he made one of the finest catches ever made until that time in World Series play, racing 420 feet to the center-field fence and making a leaping catch of the drive by Happy Felsch. In fact, had Roush's spectacular catch been filmed it would probably be acknowledged today as equal to the infamous catch made by Willie Mays in the Polo Grounds of Vic Wertz's long drive in the eighth inning of the opening game of the 1954 World Series.

The only current event other than the series that was being talked about during the delay was President Woodrow Wilson's illness. There were reports of a slight improvement in his condition, nonetheless physicians were in constant attendance at the bedside of the president and his family had been called to Washington. King Albert of Belgium decided as a result of Wilson's illness to cancel the remaining itinerary on his tour of the United States after stops in Buffalo and Boston. The stock market was somewhat wobbly due to reports of Wilson's health and the Senate had decided to go right ahead with a vote on the peace treaty including the covenant of the League of Nations.

A great number of fans waited out the rain delay by just hanging out in the hotel lobbies hoping to get a glance at some of players, be they Reds or White Sox. The rather handsome Jimmy Ring was the object of all the ladies' eyes as he walked through the lobby of the Sherman House. It was the opinion of the ladies at the Sherman House that Ring was even more handsome than Francis Bushman. Over at the Congress the bellhops constantly nagged Reds manager Pat Moran. Nonetheless, Pat did his best to remain under cover.

Bill Rariden and Edd Roush entertained fans from their hometowns of Bedford and Oakland City, Indiana. The word around the press corps was that Rariden and Roush were carrying on a dialogue with their supporters about the crops.

Heinie Groh was spending some time setting the record straight on remarks that he was supposed to have made about White Sox shortstop Swede Risberg. Sportswriter Ring Lardner reported that Groh had stated that Risberg would be sitting on the White Sox bench next year. Groh refuted these remarks by stating, "Don't take too seriously everything written about this series. I never told Risberg that. It's not my system to ride a player of the Risberg type. I prefer to pick on established stars."

In some respects it is amazing what boredom will drive people to do. Some sportswriters and fans spent time during the delay theorizing on how the rain affected the White Sox pitchers. It was felt that Grover Lowdermilk always got taller after a heavy rain, that Dickie Kerr usually gets cross and mean, while Lefty Williams just kind of smiles and makes the best of it.

Still other visiting fans and members of the press used the delay to visit Chicago restaurants and theatres and also take advantage of the wide-open bars and taverns to soothe their parched throats. National prohibition was on the horizon, but on October 5, 1919, Chicago was still a very wet town on the inside as well as the outside.

Back east baseball was continuing with a barnstorming tour by John McGraw's New York Giants who had finished second in the 1919 National League pennant race behind Pat Moran's Reds. Tomorrow on October 6, as the World Series was scheduled to resume at Comiskey Park in Chicago, at Shibe Park in Philadelphia the New York Giants were scheduled to play the Atlantic City Bacharach Giants of the Negro League. The New York Giants starting pitcher was either going to be Gene Dubuc (6-4) or Jess Barnes (25-9) who would face off against Bacharach Giants ace Dick "Cannon Ball" Redding (1919 record unknown). The game was scheduled for 3:00 P.M. and results of the fifth game of the World Series from Chicago would be posted at Shibe Park.

On Sunday, October 5, 1919, an editorial appeared in the *Philadelphia Inquirer* that read in part:

"Those who believe that politics is the one absorbing interest in the American people must not lose sight of the continued popularity of baseball.

The attendance and receipts for the World Series indicate that the game holds its own as the national pastime. Sixty thousand at the first two games and $300,000 in receipts is to say that the sport is close to the hearts of the people."[1]

Later in the day the sun came out in Chicago and the forecast was for continued clearing tomorrow and the call of play ball.

With the sun shining at Comiskey Park a record 34,379 fans were in attendance, 16 more for game five than for game four. The ticket scalpers were getting as much as $29.00 for a box seat and thousands of fans were turned away. The flags and yards of bunting were flying gracefully in the breeze and the diamond looked to be in fine shape for the game; however, the outfield was mushy in parts.

The starting pitchers for the game were Hod Eller who had won 20 games and lost 9 for the Reds in the regular season and Lefty Williams who was making his second start in the series for the White Sox. Eller would be the fifth pitcher in five games to start for Cincinnati in the series.

Eller was actually a White Sox cast-off. Four years previous he had been recruited by the White Sox but after a brief trial was sent packing being judged as not good enough. To face the White Sox as a starting pitcher in a World Series game was nothing short of sweet revenge for Eller.

Horace Eller got his nickname of Hod because he was supposed to be full of bricks that he threw at batters. Eller, like Eddie Cicotte, was known to be one of the practitioners of the infamous "shine ball."

The "shine ball" got its name from the fact that the pitcher usually rubbed the ball against his uniform prior to delivery. The ball was thrown at a speed of 70 to 80 mph and the smoothed area helped the ball slip out of the hand, therefore helping the ball to curve. Eddie Cicotte is the pitcher who first noticed that the ball would do very funny things after rubbing one side of it to a shine on his uniform, and he is given the most credit for developing the pitch.[2]

Sportswriter Grantland Rice described the "shine ball" as one that is rubbed against the trouser leg, then when it approaches the plate it "develops a glossy smoothness to the ball at the anointed spot and helps develop a hop and a jump entirely too swift for the human eye."[3]

In the first inning Morrie Rath led off the game with a walk from Williams. Jake Daubert then sacrificed and Rath took second. However, Williams closed out the first by getting Groh to fly out to Felsch and Roush to ground to Gandil who threw to Williams covering first.

In the bottom of the first Nemo Leibold also led off with a walk from Eller. Eddie Collins followed by grounding out, Kopf to Daubert, in a close play at first. Collins protested the call but to no avail. Buck Weaver then hit a hard shot back at Eller and his fingertips deflected the ball. Nemo Leibold took third on the play. But Eller was out of the inning as Joe Jackson hit a high pop fly that Groh caught on the baseline and Happy Felsch flied out to Duncan in left.

Lefty Williams set the Reds down in order with ease in the top of the second by striking out Pat Duncan, getting Kopf to foul out to Schalk and then fanning Greasy Neale.

In the bottom of the second Hod Eller struck out the side, whiffing in order Gandil, Risberg and Schalk.

Williams had no trouble retiring the Reds in the third, getting Bill Rariden to ground out to Gandil, Eller to lift a pop fly near the box caught by Weaver and then getting Rath to also hit a pop up caught by Gandil.

In the bottom of the third Eller continued his dominance of the Sox. Lefty Williams led off and was fanned. Nemo Leibold was then struck out and finally Eddie Collins also went down on strikes, becoming the sixth consecutive batter that Eller had fanned. As Eller left the mound the Chicago fans cheered him wildly. The *Baseball Encyclopedia* states "There [was] no taint on the streak: among those fanned were Schalk, Leibold and Collins."

Despite an error by Swede Risberg who let a ground ball hit by Heinie Groh go through his hands for an error, Williams had no trouble in retiring the Reds in the fourth.

In the bottom of the fourth Eller's strikeout streak came to an end as Buck Weaver leading off hit an easy taper back at him that he fielded and threw to Daubert for the out. Joe Jackson also hit a ground ball back to Eller for the second out. Happy Felsch then became Eller's seventh strikeout victim.

Williams had been pitching no-hit ball through four innings until Larry Kopf led off the fifth with a single over second base. Greasy Neale then attempted to sacrifice but hit a grounder to Risberg, who flipped the ball to Eddie Collins forcing Kopf. With Bill Rariden up, Pat Moran then called for a hit-and-run play. However, when Rariden attempted to hit he could not reach Williams' pitch and Neale was thrown out by Schalk attempting to reach second on a steal. Rariden then flied out to end the inning.

In the bottom of the fifth Gandil grounded out, Rath to Daubert, and Risberg grounded out, Groh to Daubert. Ray Schalk then got the Sox's second hit off Eller when he hit a line single to left. However, Lefty Williams followed by becoming Eller's eighth strikeout victim.

Going into the sixth inning Hod Eller and Lefty Williams had been locked in a scoreless pitching duel with the Reds getting one hit off Williams and the White Sox getting two hits off Eller.

Hod Eller was the Reds' leadoff batter in the sixth. Eller had hit .280 during the regular season having 26 hits for 93 at bats. Eller was also known as a dead pull hitter to left. Coming down the Reds' pennant-stretch drive in September, he had broke open a game in which he was pitching against the Giants at the Polo Grounds with a powerful home run far up into the left field bleachers with two men on.

Kid Gleason should have been aware of Eller's strong tendency to hit the ball to left. Nonetheless, in the first inning he had pulled Happy Felsch over towards right leaving a gap between center and left. Eller of course had popped out in his first at bat in the third. But once again with Eller leading off the sixth, Gleason waved Felsch over towards right. Eller drove the ball into left center between Jackson and Felsch. Felsch chased the ball down as it rolled toward the fence and then made a high throw to Risberg. Risberg deflected the ball and it rolled away from him allowing Eller to race for third with credit for a double and third on the error.

In the opinion of sportswriter Grantland Rice, "Had Risberg not deflected the throw and left the play alone the ball would have traveled directly to Buck Weaver waiting on the bag."[4]

Morrie Rath was next and crossed up the entire Sox team by unleashing a single to right that scored Eller.

Jake Daubert sacrificed Rath to second. Williams then attempted to dust off Heinie Groh before walking him on the next four pitches.

Then for some unknown reason Happy Felsch moved into short center field with a long-ball hitter in Edd Roush coming to bat. Williams once again came in close on the batter with his first pitch and Roush took exception to Williams attempting to hit him with the ball. Roush shouted out to Williams on the mound, "Pitch the ball through here and I'll knock it down your throat." On the next pitch Roush quickly hit an easy fly to center where Felsch misjudged it, running in on a ball that was over his head. Felsch then raced back and attempted to make the catch over his head, but the ball bounced out of his hands as he slipped and fell. Roush raced around the bases for a triple in what should have been an easy out. Of course Rath scored easily on the play. When Felsch had both recovered his balance and the ball, he threw it in to Eddie Collins who unleashed a low throw towards the plate in a hurried attempt to get Groh. As Groh was tearing toward the plate, Ray Schalk had to reach forward to take the throw from Collins and failed to tag Groh who also scored.

When home plate National League umpire Cy Rigler called Groh safe it sent Schalk into a rage! He hurled insults and expletives at Rigler and the entire Cincinnati team, then jumped over Groh and attempted to get at Rigler. He pushed Rigler with considerable force and was immediately ejected from the game. At this point Reds pitcher Jimmy Ring came running out of the Cincinnati dugout to assist Rigler. Schalk then threw his mask at Ring hitting him in the kneecap. Umpire Rigler then started pulling Schalk away from the fray. Angrily, Schalk retired to the Chicago dugout. Rigler also ejected Reds thirdbase coach Jimmy Smith from the game for his behavior in the incident along the baseline.

Heinie Groh remarked after the game, "Schalk didn't tag me and should not have kicked so much. I slid in with my arms outstretched and my hand brushed the plate as he came down with the ball — and missed me. [Buck] Weaver later told me he was sure Schalk had not tagged me. I know he didn't."[5]

Reserve catcher Byrd Lynn replaced Schalk behind the plate and play was resumed. Pat Duncan hit a sacrifice fly to Joe Jackson; Roush scored the fourth Cincinnati run of the inning as Lynn fumbled a throw made to the plate by Jackson. Larry Kopf then flied out to Felsch, ending the innings.

The Reds had once again made maximum use of all their base runners, getting four runs on three hits. Unfortunately, Gleason's ill-conceived strategy in moving his outfielders and Felsch's bad play in the field broke up one of the most exciting pitching duels in World Series history up to that time between Eller and Williams.

In the bottom of the sixth Eller set the White Sox down in order. Nemo Leibold grounded out, Eddie Collins flied out and Buck Weaver hit a hot grounder to Kopf who tossed to Daubert for the out.

Despite a four-run deficit Lefty Williams continued pitching brilliantly, setting the Reds down in order in the top of the seventh getting Neale to ground out, Rariden to fly out and striking out Eller.

In the bottom of the seventh Eller also set the White Sox down in order. Jackson grounded out, Rath to Daubert. Happy Felsch then came up and after swinging at and missing one of Eller's pitches, he picked the ball up and examined it, attempting to see what the Reds hurler had smeared on its surface. A fan in the grandstand yelled at Happy, "Yes it's a baseball, you're supposed to hit it."[6] Felsch then hit a high foul ball that Rariden caught near the Chicago dugout. Gandil ended the inning flying out to Roush.

In the top of the eighth Williams once again set the Reds down in order. Rath flied out to Jackson, both Daubert and Groh flied out to Felsch. Williams had set down the last seven Reds batters to face him.

Eller continued his dominance over the Sox in the bottom of the eighth getting Risberg to line to Neale, Byrd Lynn to fly out to Duncan and striking out Eddie Murphy who was sent up to pinch-hit for Lefty Williams. Murphy was Eller's ninth strike out and tenth man in a row that he had retired.

Erskine Mayer was sent in by Kid Gleason to pitch the ninth inning for the White Sox. The White Sox obtained Mayer from the Pittsburgh Pirates on waivers in August 1919. Previously Mayer had two 20-game-win seasons while pitching for the Philadelphia Phillies in 1914 (21-19) and 1915 (21-15).

Edd Roush led off and hit a grounder to Eddie Collins, who bobbled it allowing Roush to be safe at first. Mayer then walked Pat Duncan. With runners on first and second, Larry Kopf laid down a sacrifice moving the runners over to second and third. Greasy Neale then hit a slow roller to Risberg. On Risberg's throw to first for the out, Roush raced for home from third scoring the Reds fifth run. Rariden then grounded out.

In the bottom of the ninth Eller got the first two hitters out, both Leibold and Collins grounding out. Buck Weaver then hit a two-out triple to right center between Roush and Neale. However, as one writer put it, Weaver then went right from third to the clubhouse as Joe Jackson grounded out, Kopf to Daubert, to end the game.

Had the owners and leagues not expanded the World Series in 1919 from seven to nine games it would have been curtains right here for the White Sox, and the Reds would have trotted back to Cincinnati World Champions winning the series 4-1. The entire conspiracy argument as well would have been a lot harder to sell as the Reds shutout the White Sox in both games four and five with all of the alleged nonconspirators making absolutely no contribution to the White Sox efforts. But with a nine game series the Sox were still alive and game five only the latest result.

In pitching the third consecutive shutout in the series, Hod Eller threw a masterpiece. He gave up only three hits and struck out nine, while walking just one batter. So in control was Eller that the White Sox did not get a runner past second base until there were two outs in the ninth inning.

His six consecutive strikeouts in the second and third innings had not been done before in the World Series. However, his nine strikeouts for the game were not a series record at the time as Big Ed Walsh, the White Sox spitball artist, had 12 strikeouts against the Chicago Cubs in the third game of the 1906 World Series. Likewise, Bill Donovan pitching for Detroit had fanned 12 Cubs in the first game of the 1907 World Series that went 12 innings and ended in a 3-3 tie. Bill Dineen pitching for the Pittsburgh Pirates had 11 strikeouts against Boston in the 1903 World Series and several pitchers had 10 strikeouts in a series game.

Following game five sportswriter Grantland Rice wrote, "On the day before the game Christy Mathweson made this remark:

"'Eller tomorrow will cut loose a shine ball far beyond anything Eddie Cicotte ever knew in the way of shinning the pill.' Was Matty correct? Ask Eddie Collins, Joe Jackson, Hap Felsch, Chick Gandil or any other member of the White Sox crew. If they care to speak what they know to be true deep down in their disheartened souls, they will tell you Eller had more stuff than they had ever faced before.

"The score tells part of it, but not even a three hit shutout quite outlines the utter helplessness of a club that batted .287 against the various staffs of the American League."[7]

Reds Captain and third baseman Heinie Groh said after the game that he heard Chick Gandil say, "You can't hit that kind of pitching." Furthermore, Groh states that Joe Jackson told some of the Reds players, "That both Ring and Eller had more smoke than [Walter] Johnson."[8]

Lefty Williams actually pitched a very good game for Chicago. He was locked in a scoreless duel with Eller through five innings. He only gave up four hits in eight innings and his pitching was far from what one would expect from an alleged conspirator. If it were not for the two hits that Felsch misplayed in the sixth as a result of Gleason's ill-conceived strategy to move him toward right and open a gap in left center, Williams would have been able to retire the Reds without a run.

Following the White Sox loss in the fifth game, manager Kid Gleason was coming under fire in the press and Jim Nasium of the *Philadelphia Inquirer* offered this analysis of Gleason's managerial abilities.

> The White Sox have been spilling as much of the dope in this series as have the Reds. They were thought to have possessed a powerful attack and it has proved to be feeble as a tottering centenarian from the blind asylum. They were generally supposed to have had a weak pitching staff and if they lost the series, it had been doped that they would lose through pitching weakness, but the pitching of the Sox pitchers has been sensational except for the first start made by Cicotte.
>
> They were supposed to have a wise and cagey manager, but throughout this series Gleason has shown that he has either been totally careless and negligent in obtaining his advance dope on the Cincinnati players or else he doesn't know how to handle a ball club for an important series, and he has continually gummed his attack by resorting to old stuff that died as a baseball strategy when the gray-haired kid was a pup.
>
> The White Sox defeat in this series cannot be charged to the failure of their pitching, which has been wonderful. It has resulted from nothing else but miserable management, poor judgment in playing Cincinnati hitters, lack of guts in the White Sox lineup and the fact that they are facing in this Cincinnati ball club one of the greatest World's Series ball clubs that the game has known in recent years — a club that is great in that it produces its best work in the crucial situations and never needs but one opportunity to slam in the winning margin.[9]

The last few words of the last sentence written by Nasium effectively tell the story of the Reds' victories in the first five games of the series and anyone convinced of the impact of a conspiracy is going to be hard pressed to deny the fact that the Reds hit when it counted. They took full advantage of almost every opportunity to score and then notwithstanding the first-game blowout of the White Sox, their defense and pitching made the runs stand up for the margin of victory. So far in the series the Reds had made 30 hits and the White Sox 29, yet the Reds were now leading the series 4-1. And after five games now, the White Sox had still only produced one earned run.

Sportswriter Hugh Fullerton, who had been so arrogant and sure of the White Sox' dominance over the Reds before the series began, was now being lampooned in cartoons in various newspapers with blurbs like "Wonder what Hugh Fullerton's alibi will be for that line of dope of his?"[10] Following the series Fullerton, with his reputation on the line, would doggedly pursue the conspiracy angle to recover his honor and to downplay to the hilt all of the superior play of the Reds in the series.

Heinie Groh remarking on the glee in the Reds clubhouse following game five stated that, "We Reds thought we were happy in the clubhouse after the game, until Bill Killefer and Grover Cleveland Alexander came in. Then we knew our joy was tame. Why those two great players were so happy they were crying. They have pulled for us and helped us every minute of the way. I can't thank them too much."[11]

The Reds were now very confident that they were about to put the White Sox out of their misery in the series. There was even a cocky air to their posture as they slapped each other on the back and gave assurances that by this time tomorrow they would be champions of the world.

Groh reported in his column for the *Cincinnati Post* that after the game, "All the Reds pitchers wanted a crack at the Sox. Eddy Gerner our young southpaw, who started only one National League game this year, said in the clubhouse after Monday's game that he was entitled to the honor of hurling the next game. Larry Kopf silenced him with a remark that he, Kopf, was going to pitch and that Gerner could play short.

"Rube Bressler and Adolfo Luque were wild to pitch. Jimmy Ring and Ray Fisher each wanted another shot at the Sox batters before they got out of range and so did Walter Ruether and Slim Sallee. Roy Mitchell claimed he was entitled to due consideration, I'm glad Pat Moran has to pick the pitcher and not me."[12]

However, it certainly did look like the White Sox were on the ropes now, down 4-1 in the best of nine series. As for the betting elements, it was suddenly difficult to find any money being bet on the White Sox in game six to be played in Cincinnati tomorrow.

For the owners and players alike the record gate made it a sure thing that the 1919 World Series was going to be a lucrative event. After five games the total attendance was 158,069 producing gross receipts of $482,229. To date the players' share stood at $260,349.66, the owners' and leagues' share at $174,566.40, and the National Commission's share at $48,212.90.

Following game five special trains were prepared to transport the teams, sportswriters and fans to Cincinnati. Most of the sportswriters were hopeful that they would not have to endure a return night ride to Chicago and that Cincinnati would take one of the next two games scheduled there and bring the whole affair to an end.

Box Score Game Five

Cincinnati	ab	r	h	rbi	Chicago	ab	r	h	rbi
Rath, 2b	3	1	1	1	Leibold, rf	3	0	0	0
Daubert, 1b	2	0	0	0	E. Collins, 2b	4	0	0	0
Groh, 3b	3	1	0	0	Weaver, 3b	4	0	2	0
Roush, cf	4	2	1	2	Jackson. lf	4	0	0	0
Duncan, lf	2	0	0	1	Felsch, cf	3	0	0	0
Kopf, ss	3	0	1	0	Gandil, 1b	3	0	0	0
Neale, rf	4	0	0	1	Risberg, ss	3	0	0	0
Rariden, c	4	0	0	0	Schalk, c	2	0	1	0
Eller, p	3	1	1	0	Williams, p	2	0	0	0
					Murphy, ph	1	0	0	0
					Mayer, p	0	0	0	0

Cincinnati	ip	h	r	er	bb	so
Eller	9	3	0	0	1	9

Chicago						
Williams	8	4	4	4	2	3
Mayer	1	0	1	0	1	0

LOB Cincinnati 3, Chicago 4, E E. Collins, H. Felsch, S. Risberg, 2b Eller, 3b Roush, Weaver, S Daubert 2, Kopf, SB Roush

CHAPTER SEVEN

Game Six

At Cincinnati, October 7, 1919

	1	2	3	4	5	6	7	8	9	10	R	H	E
Chicago	0	0	0	0	1	3	0	0	0	1	5	10	3
Cincinnati	0	0	2	2	0	0	0	0	0	0	4	11	0

Kerr
Ruether, Ring (6)

After an all-night ride down from Chicago in Pullman cars, "rattlers" as Heinie Groh called them, the Reds and White Sox arrived in Cincinnati for game six.

Most observers felt that the end of the series would come today; if not, tomorrow for sure. A sell-out crowd of 32,006 turned out at Redland Field for what the Reds faithful hoped would be the "coup de grace" on the mighty White Sox in the World Series.

In hopes that he could stay alive in the series, Kid Gleason selected Dickie Kerr as the White Sox starting pitcher. Kerr was making his second start following his masterful 3-0 shutout of the Reds in game three. Also, Kerr would work with three days rest.

For the Reds Pat Moran elected to go with Dutch Ruether who also was making his second start in the series following his 9-1 drubbing of the Sox in game one.

The umpires took up their positions with Billy Evans, the dean of American League umpires, working behind the plate, Rigler at third, Nallin at second and Quigley at first. The sixth game of the series was underway.

John "Shano" Collins led off the sixth game for the White Sox. Collins took Ruether to a full count before flying out to Roush. Eddie Collins also flied out to Roush. With two outs Buck Weaver continued his hot hitting in the series by hitting the ball just out of reach of Kopf for a single. However, Joe Jackson ended the inning by popping out to Groh.

In the bottom of the first after Larry Rath popped out to Risberg and Daubert grounded out, Heinie Groh lined the ball into right field for a double. Roush then hit the ball in the direction of Risberg who knocked it down as the ball rolled toward first. Groh, running into third, overran the bag and Risberg gunned him down a foot from the bag with a quick throw to Weaver.

Ruether set the Sox down in order in the second.

In the bottom of the second the Reds again attempted to rally. Pat Duncan led off and hit an easy grounder to Risberg who stopped the ball then fumbled the throw. Kerr then walked Larry Kopf. Greasy Neale attempted to sacrifice but instead hit a bounder back at Kerr. Only 5'7", Kerr had to jump to field the ball, but then threw to Weaver at third forcing Duncan. Bill Rariden then hit a grounder to Eddie Collins who threw to second forcing Neale. However, Neale slid into Risberg, breaking up the double play as Swede fell over him. Rariden was safe at first. But the inning ended as Dutch Ruether hit a weak ball back to Kerr who threw to Gandil for the out.

In the third after Ruether walked Ray Schalk, Dickie Kerr laid down a perfect sacrifice and Schalk went to second. However, both Shano Collins and Eddie Collins flied out.

In the bottom of the third the Reds finally scored some runs off of Dickie Kerr after he had shut them out for 11 innings in the series. After Morrie Rath led off by grounding out, Jake Daubert singled to right. Heinie Groh was then called out on strikes, but Jake Daubert stole second. Kerr then plucked Edd Roush in the ribs with an inshoot. Roush took first. With two men on and two out, Pat Duncan hit a liner to deep center that scored both Duncan and Roush. Duncan pulled up at third. However, Larry Kopf followed by hitting a fly deep to center that was caught by Felsch.

In the top of the fourth after Buck Weaver flied out to deep center and Joe Jackson hit a pop foul behind the plate caught by Rariden, Happy Felsch drove a single to left. Gandil followed by grounding out, Kopf to Daubert.

In the bottom of the fourth the Reds went after Kerr again and the fans started to sense victory and the World Championship. Greasy Neale led off with a triple to deep center. Dutch Ruether, who had three hits in the first game, then hit the ball hard across the third-base bag, which then curved into the temporary stands for a double. Neale scored the Reds' third run on Ruether's hit. Larry Rath then grounded to Risberg, who attempted to throw Ruether out going into third, but the ball hit him in the shoulder. As the ball rolled away, Ruether scored the Reds' fourth run of the game. Rath took second on the play and then moments later steals third. Jake Daubert then hit a short fly to left that was caught by Jackson. Rath breaks for the plate and is cut down by Jackson's throw.

This particular play to end the bottom of the fourth is more grist for the mill in the continuing controversy over the series. For some unknown reason, a lot of people who continue to analyze the 1919 World Series in the new millennium believe that the throw from Jackson was wide, but after catching the ball Schalk threw himself between the plate and Rath to make the tag. One can find this account of the play in an unusual amount of Internet website articles on the 1919 World Series.

Respected sportswriter Ren Mulford, Jr., who was an eyewitness to the play, reported it in his postgame column this way. "He [Rath] tried to score after Daubert's fly to left but Jackson *cut him down by a great throw to Schalk*."[1]

Year 2000 reports on plays involving Shoeless Joe Jackson as opposed to eyewitness reports from 1919 try to keep the conspiracy theory alive undermining every creditable play in the field involving him. Due to the fact that Joe Jackson hit .375 in the series, there is not much room for discrediting the intensity of his play other than by distorting the facts. If one loses the luxury of indicting Joe Jackson in advancing the conspiracy theory, then they have lost the argument of the conspiracy having any serious consequences on the outcome of the series. Without Jackson the Cicotte, Felsch, Gandil, Risberg, Williams connection will not stand up to scrutiny.

In the top of the fifth the White Sox battled back. Swede Risberg led off with a walk and Ray Schalk did the same. Dickie Kerr then hit the ball to Kopf, who knocked it down but couldn't make the play. Risberg overran third and Kopf threw the ball to Groh, but he failed to make the tag. With bases loaded and no one out, Roush was playing in tight behind second and made an easy catch of Shano Collins' shallow fly ball back of second. The runners all held their bases.

Eddie Collins then hit a sacrifice fly to Roush, scoring Risberg with the White Sox's first run in the last 26 innings off of Reds pitching.

Joe Jackson, probably 1915 when he was purchased by the Sox. (ICHI-27160; Chicago Historical Society; SDN-58463-A. Photography: *Chicago Daily News*).

Ray Schalk did not attempt to advance to third. Consequently, Kerr ran towards second not realizing that Schalk was still there. Heinie Groh, who had received the ball back in the infield from Roush, ran all the way across the diamond and tagged Kerr for the out completing the double play.

Kerr set down the Reds one, two, three in the bottom of the fifth as Groh, Roush and Duncan all flied out.

Behind in the game 4-1 Chicago had its biggest inning of the series so far in the top of the sixth scoring three runs.

Buck Weaver led off and hit a fly ball to left that Duncan and Kopf let fall between them for a double. Though Duncan and Kopf maintained that due to the crowd noise they could not hear each other yell for the ball, it was a huge miscue and the beginning of the end for the Reds in game six.

Joe Jackson followed with a single over second scoring Weaver. Happy Felsch then doubled to left scoring Jackson. At that point for some reason Reds manager Pat Moran decided that Ruether had enough for the day and brought in Jimmy Ring to pitch. Ring had started and won game four with a five-hit shutout 2-0.

Ring quickly got Chick Gandil to pop out to Daubert and Risberg to ground out, Rath to Daubert. Happy Felsch took third on the play on Risberg. Ray Schalk then hit a single driving in Felsch with the tying run. Schalk then stole second, but died there as Kerr grounded out, Groh to Daubert.

Heinie Groh remarked after the game about the White Sox sudden comeback in the sixth inning. "I never saw a ball club that had as much at stake show such a reversal of spirit and form in one afternoon as the Sox did in today's game. They were licked in the third and fourth innings and knew it. There didn't seem to be any fight left in them. It looked as if we would make a million runs. But when we gave them an opening in the sixth they stole our stuff and grabbed the chance. All of a sudden they were the kind of a club they must have been when they ripped along to the American League pennant."[2]

In the bottom of the sixth Greasy Neale led off with a single off of Kerr's glove. However, Bill Rariden followed by lining out to Shano Collins, Jimmy Ring struck out and Neale was thrown out by Schalk attempting to steal second.

In the top of the seventh with the score deadlocked at 4-4, the White Sox manager sent the right-hand hitting Nemo Leibold up to hit for Shano Collins. Leibold promptly grounded out, Kopf to Daubert. Eddie Collins then hit a high fly to Roush and Buck Weaver grounded out, Rath to Daubert.

Once again the Reds got the leadoff batter aboard in the bottom of the seventh when Morrie Rath singled. Jake Daubert then laid down a sacrifice and Rath went to second. Kerr walked Heinie Groh. But the rally fizzled when Edd Roush followed by hitting into a double play.

The score remained tied at 4-4 in the top of the eighth as Joe Jackson opened the inning with a walk. Happy Felsch then flied out to Neale. Ring then walked Chick Gandil on four straight pitches. With two men on and one out, Swede Risberg hit a low liner to center that the speedy Edd Roush raced in on and made a shoestring catch. Roush then quickly threw to Rath at second for a double play on Jackson.

In the Reds' half of the eighth Kerr got the leadoff batter, Pat Duncan, to foul out to Gandil who made the catch running back near the field boxes.

Larry Kopf then hit a hot liner back at Kerr that he caught even though it literally blistered the fingers on his pitching hand. After a brief time out, Kid Gleason left Kerr in the game. Greasy Neale stepped up to the plate and hit a single. Bill Rariden then got an infield hit.

For some unknown reason with two men on, two outs and possibly the World Championship on the line, Reds manager Pat Moran then elected to allow weak-hitting pitcher Jimmy Ring to face Kerr. Ring hit the ball to Risberg, forcing Rariden at second to end the inning.

The tie ball game moved into the ninth inning and Ray Schalk led off for the Sox and Ring struck him out. Dickie Kerr then hit the ball back to Ring who threw Daubert for the second out. Nemo Leibold kept the White Sox's hopes alive with a walk, but Eddie Collins, continuing to struggle in the series at bat, flied out to Roush.

Dickie Kerr continued on the hill for the White Sox and got Morrie Rath to ground out to open the bottom of the ninth. Jake Daubert then drove a clean single into center, the Reds' 11th hit in the game off Kerr. But the Reds' chances of wrapping up the series quickly died as Heinie Groh forced Daubert, Risberg to Collins. With Roush at bat, Groh attempted to steal and was thrown out by Schalk.

As play moved into the top of the tenth inning, the first extra-inning game of the series, the Reds just seemed to implode.

Buck Weaver led off and hit a short fly to left that bounded away from Duncan and went for two bases. Joe Jackson followed by laying down a bunt that Rariden could not get a good handle on. With Jackson on first and Weaver on third, Ring struck out Felsch for the first out. Chick Gandil then hit a high-bounding grounder that scored Weaver with the go ahead run for the Sox. However, the rally quickly died as Risberg lined to Kopf who doubled up Jackson at second.

This was the second time in the last three innings that Jackson had been doubled up at second base on a ball hit by Risberg. Of course it can happen to any base runner, but with so much on the line and only one out it brings into focus how careless Jackson's lead off the bases must have been in this situation. Nonetheless, those who are convinced of the conspiracy and Jackson's alleged participation have never called this game six situation into question. I suppose that when the White Sox are winning a game in the series that bad base running by any of the White Sox players is purely coincidental and not intentional to those convinced of a fix.

In the bottom of the tenth the Reds folded like cardboard as Kerr set the Reds down in order. Edd Roush grounded out, Pat Duncan fouled out behind the plate and Larry Kopf grounded out, Collins to Gandil, for the final out.

The game had taken two hours and six minutes to play, the Reds had blown an opportunity to wrap up the series and now there would be a seventh game tomorrow.

Rookie Dickie Kerr was far from being as effective as he had been in game three, but he went the distance and more, pitching ten innings and giving up 11 hits, while winning his second game in the series.

Sportswriter Ren Mulford, Jr., wrote in the *Cincinnati Post* following the game, "Dick Kerr did not pitch world championship ball. But he lasted. Instead of making five out of six, those Reds of ours failed to clinch the big prize. They lost in the first extra inning contest of the series, when they should have had it salted away in the old pork barrel well before the end of the ninth."[3]

The Reds had Dickie Kerr beat in the bottom of the eighth inning. The shot that Larry Kopf hit back at Kerr bruised his pitching hand when he caught it. He then proceeded to give up back to back two-out singles to Neale and Rariden. Kid Gleason was so concerned that Kerr may have been through he quickly began warming up Big Bill James.

But then Pat Moran made a gift of game six to the White Sox with a strategy that is totally illogical under the circumstances. With the score tied 4-4, two out and two on, with the 1919 World Championship on the line, Moran neglected to pinch-hit for Jimmy Ring. Jimmy Ring was not known as a hitting pitcher. In fact, going into the series he had a lifetime batting average of just .104 (14 for 132) and would end his career with an average of .147 (120 for 817). This move by Moran becomes even more bizarre when one considers that he had pinch hitters available for duty such as Sherry Magee, a former National League batting champion, and Rube Bressler, a player who would eventually have a lifetime batting average of .301 for 19 years in the big leagues. Both Magee and Bressler were right-handed hitters that could face the left-handed Kerr.

Ring comes up to bat, fails to hit the ball out of the infield and the Reds blow an opportunity to finish off the White Sox in the series. Consequently, Moran's illogical strategy and a twist in fate allow Dickie Kerr, who pitched a mediocre game, to become a 1919 World Series hero and undeserved icon.

Ring's hitting aside, he did not do poorly in his relief appearance and pitched five strong innings, giving up four hits and one run.

As for Reds starting pitcher Dutch Ruether who was so effective against the Sox in game one, he just did not have the same stuff on the ball in game six. However, he continued to hit with authority in the series, going one for two with an extra-base hit and a RBI, while raising his batting average to a blazing .667.

There is of course another angle to the Reds' loss in game six. Heinie Groh pointed out following the game that the fatal mistake that beat the Reds may have been in the top of the sixth when Larry Kopf and Pat Duncan let Buck Weaver's fly ball between them for a double. Following that faux pas Joe Jackson singled scoring Weaver, and the White Sox rally began that brought three Sox across the plate erasing the Reds 4-1 lead.

Cincinnati Post sportswriter Tom Swope agreed with Groh. "Larry Kopf or Pat Duncan, or both of them prevented the Reds from winning their fifth victory Tuesday and ending the series in six games. They let a fly ball drop safe between them that one of them should have caught."[4]

Groh also offered some other reasons for the Reds' loss that seem a bit unusual to those of us looking at these events 81 years later. Nonetheless, the environment of baseball that players labored in then was far different from that of major league baseball today. Groh stated that he thought the loss in game six was due in part to the Reds' travel arrangements following game five in Chicago.

"We took the field following a night on the train. Don't tell me that the Sox had the same handicap, I know it. But I also know the only two games we have lost in this World Series took place a few hours after we hopped off Pullmans. If we had to ride trains every night I feel sure we wouldn't win many games. Our club is composed of players who just don't take to this business of sleeping on the rattlers. [Dutch] Ruether, I believe, had too much rest before going to the hill. He had rested five full days."[5]

If there is any irony to game six it is that alleged conspirator Chick Gandil kept the White Sox alive in the series by knocking in the winning run in the top of the tenth inning.

This one event tends to pour ice water on the conspiracy angle. As for the take-no-prisoners conspiracy devotees from Hugh Fullerton to Eliot Asinof to Ward and Burns and thousands of others, Gandil's action in the sixth game weakens their arguments as to the intensity of the fix. It certainly brings credence to Edd Roush's assertion stated earlier that when the White Sox players did not get their money after the first game, they tried to win the series. No one, be they a proponent of the conspiracy theory or the Reds' superiority, ever even remotely suggests that Gandil's effort in game six was anything other than legitimate.

One more loss in the series would have meant that the White Sox were defeated. Therefore, it was time for Gandil, if he were still in on the fix, to take the money and run. What sense would it had made for Gandil to drive in a winning run if he was still pursuing ways to lose ball games in the series? When he came to bat in the top of the tenth with hard-throwing Jimmy Ring on the mound, no one would have questioned it if he had fouled off a couple of pitches, taken a strike or swung right through one of Ring's fastballs and struck out. Instead Gandil makes contact with the ball, and the result is ultimately the winning run and the margin that keeps the Sox alive in the series.

The sixth game certainly was keeping the baseball bean counters alive too. After six games the record series attendance was now 190,075 and gross receipts had ballooned to $583,896.36. The players' share, which did not continue to escalate after the fifth game, was $260,349.06.

So there was more revenue to come as the Reds' victory champagne was not yet on ice. However, one anonymous Red told the press it was there behind a swinging door in the clubhouse, that is now nailed shut. "As soon as we cinch the series, if we end it at home, we'll kick that door wide open and go for that stuff."

However, that action would be delayed, even further.

Box Score Game Six

Chicago	ab	r	h	rbi	Cincinnati	ab	r	h	rbi
S. Collins, rf	3	0	0	0	Rath, 2b	5	0	1	1
Leibold, rf	1	0	0	0	Daubert, 1b	4	1	2	0
E. Collins, 2b	4	0	0	1	Groh, 3b	4	0	1	0
Weaver, 3b	5	2	3	0	Roush, cf	4	1	1	0
Jackson, lf	4	1	2	1	Duncan, lf	5	0	1	2
Felsch, cf	5	1	2	1	Kopf, ss	4	0	0	0
Gandil, 1b	4	0	1	1	Neale, rf	4	1	3	0
Risberg, ss	4	1	0	0	Rariden, c	4	0	1	0
Schalk, c	2	0	1	1	Ruether, p	2	1	1	1
Kerr, p	3	0	1	0	Ring, p	2	0	0	0

Chicago	ip	h	r	er	bb	so
Kerr	10	11	4	3	2	2

Cincinnati						
Ruether	5	6	4	4	3	0
Ring	5	4	1	1	3	2

LOB Chicago 8, Cincinnati 8, E Felsch, Risberg (2), 2B Groh, Ruether, Weaver (2), Felsch, 3b Neale, S Kerr, Daubert, E. Collins, SB Daubert, Rath, Schalk, Leibold, HBP Kerr

CHAPTER EIGHT

Game Seven

At Cincinnati, October 8, 1919

	1	2	3	4	5	6	7	8	9	R	H	E
Chicago	1	0	1	0	2	0	0	0	0	4	10	1
Cincinnati	0	0	0	0	0	1	0	0	0	1	7	4

Cicotte
Sallee, Fisher (5), Luque (6)

Gary Herrmann and the Reds front office caused a mess worse than men eating pizza at a poker game with the ticket sales for game seven. That the Reds did not wrap up the World Series in game six was a huge disappointment to the Cincinnati faithful. As all of Cincinnati, including the Reds' ownership, was so confident that there would be no seventh game, tickets had only been sold for the first three games in Cincinnati and no provisions had been made for ticket sales for a fourth game. The overnight arrangements made to allow fans to purchase tickets proved terribly inadequate. First of all, no one seemed to know where the tickets would be sold. Second, Redland Field was set deep inside Cincinnati's dowdy old West End neighborhood, far from the city center and not exactly a desirable place to be at night, even in 1919.

Despite the fact that the Reds still led the series 4-2 and with a victory in game seven would put the lid on the White Sox, the smallest crowd so far to attend a game in the series (13,923) showed up at Redland Field for game seven.

The prevailing attitude was that Cincinnati fans had not given up on the series following Tuesday's game. Most thought the sparse crowd was a result of fans not knowing how to get single game tickets due to the poor plan the Reds organization had adopted for distributing them.

Even though tickets were still plentiful on the morning of game seven, it was reported in the *Cincinnati Post* that revenue officers were on the trail of ticket scalpers. A Newark, Ohio, man was taken into custody prior to the game for selling a brace of $2.20 tickets for $11.00. The sale was made to revenue officers in a hotel lobby. The scalper was brought before the bar of justice, but due to undisclosed extenuating circumstances, he was fined $25.00 and permitted to go.

Cincinnati school children were still very much excited about the series, so for the second day in a row, principals in Cincinnati public schools dismissed school an hour early.

Not many White Sox rooters, perhaps a hundred, made the trip from Chicago back down to Cincinnati. White Sox president Charles Comiskey had a small party with him, but the majority of White Sox fans had kind of thrown in the towel after game five with the Sox on the verge of elimination 4-1.

The starting pitchers for game seven were Eddie Cicotte for the White Sox and Slim Sallee for the Reds. Cicotte was making his third start in the series having taken the loss in the opening game 9-1, then losing a pitchers' battle with Jimmy Ring in game four 2-0. Sallee had started and won game two 4-2.

The *Cincinnati Post* reported that the southpaw's arm was rested and ready to pitch the Reds to the World Championship. However, other members of the press were wondering why Reds manager Pat Moran had not elected to start Adolpho Luque rather than Sallee.

Moran had already started off the day with some bad luck. As he was traveling from his downtown Cincinnati hotel out to Redland Field he lost a gold watch and a diamond studded charm. The jewelry had been gifts from The Knights of Columbus. Now Moran was to experience some additional bad luck in game seven.

A conference between members of both teams and umpires at the plate delayed the start of the game until four minutes past two o'clock when plate umpire Quigley yelled "Play ball!"

As Nemo Leibold had very little success with the bat against left handers, Shano Collins once again got the call to start for the Sox in right field. Collins led off by fouling the first pitch from Sallee over the roof of the grandstand back of third base, before ripping a clean single past Kopf into left field. Eddie Collins then sacrificed and Shano Collins went to second.

Buck Weaver fouled several pitches off including two into the left field pavilion. Wingo then headed for the mound to talk with Sallee. On the next pitch Weaver hit a fly to deep center caught by Roush, his 28th put-out in the series.

Joe Jackson then singled to center, scoring Shano Collins from second as the small band of White Sox supporters in the stands went into a frenzy!

However, Jackson overran the bag and was caught in a run-down between first and second. He was saved by scurrying back to the bag on his stomach when Jake Daubert fumbled a throw from Morrie Rath. Reporters and others traveling with the teams after seeing the Reds infielders miss the mark on an easy out and see Jackson crawl on his stomach to reach the bag with the tips of his fingers conceded that it was time to make train accommodations for the return trip to Chicago.

Happy Felsch followed with a safe bunt, Jackson taking second. However, the rally fell short as Chick Gandil forced Felsch.

Morrie Rath led off for the Reds and hit a grounder that Cicotte let go through his legs for an error. But Cicotte then set the Reds down in order. Jake Daubert popped out to Eddie Collins, Heinie Groh struck out and Edd Roush forced Rath, Collins to Risberg.

Slim Sallee looked strong in the second as he retired the White Sox with just five pitches. Swede Risberg grounded out, Ray Schalk was out on a fly ball to right and Eddie Cicotte grounded out on an easy roller to Groh.

In the Cincinnati half of the second, after retiring Duncan on a fly ball to center, Cicotte then gave up a single to Larry Kopf. Greasy Neale then fouled out to Weaver and Kopf attempted to steal second and was thrown out.

Chicago added another run in the third as Shano Collins led off with his second hit. Eddie Collins then beat out a grounder that Kopf couldn't reach in time. Shano Collins went to second. Buck Weaver then tapped the ball to Kopf, who stepped on second forcing Eddie Collins. Kopf then began arguing that Eddie Collins interfered with his throw to first in an attempt to double up Weaver and umpire Rigler agreed with him, ordering Weaver out. With Shano Collins on third, Joe Jackson then got his second hit of the game and Collins scored. Happy Felsch then forced Jackson, Kopf to Rath, ending the Sox half of the inning.

Ivy Wingo led off the Reds third and walked. Slim Sallee then flied out to Felsch over in right field on the foul line. Morrie Rath then forced Wingo, Risberg to Eddie Collins. Jack Daubert ended the inning by hitting the ball back to Cicotte, who made a one-hand catch and tossed to Gandil at first for the out.

Sallee got the first two Sox batters out as Gandil flied out to Neale and Risberg fouled out to Daubert. Then Ray Schalk hit a smash down towards third that Groh couldn't handle in time to throw him out. But Eddie Collins followed with a deep fly to center hauled in by Roush.

Eddie Cicotte again had an easy time retiring the Reds in the fifth as they failed to get the ball out of the infield. Groh, Roush and Duncan all grounded out.

Slim Sallee got the leadoff batter out in the top of fifth as Shano Collins flew out to Neale in right.

But then the Sox went to work on him quickly. Eddie Collins hit a single into center, his second hit of the game. Buck Weaver then hit a hot smash toward third that Groh fumbled then made a high throw for an error. With Eddie Collins on second and Weaver on first, Joe Jackson hit a grounder to Rath that hit him on the ankle and bounded away, loading the bases with one out.

Happy Felsch then singled into center, scoring Eddie Collins and Buck Weaver with the Sox's third and fourth runs of the game.

Reds manager Pat Moran had been sitting in the dugout studying the ground and tearing up paper into little strips. It became apparent to him that the Reds were crumbling under the heavy attack launched on them while Sallee was on the mound. So at this juncture Moran headed out to the mound to relieve Sallee. The *Cincinnati Post* described Moran as the picture of depression. When Sallee walked to the bench he sat alongside of Moran, but there wasn't any indication of the two falling into immediate conversation.

Ray Fisher, who had started game three, was summoned from the bullpen and he finished the inning without any further trouble. He got Chick Gandil to ground out; however, both Jackson and Felsch advanced to second and third on the play. Fisher then struck out Swede Risberg to end the inning.

From the first pitch of the game, the Reds bench had been razzing the White Sox; and it intensified as Larry Kopf led off the bottom of the fifth and flied out to Jackson. Greasy Neale then singled to left and Ivy Wingo was walked. With runners on first and second and one out, Ray Fisher walked up to the plate to hit, but Moran called him back. The hot-hitting Dutch Ruether was sent up to pinch-hit for Fisher. Ruether, although a pitcher, was hitting .800 in the series (4 for 5). However, Ruether fouled out to Weaver. It was up to Morrie Rath to keep the Reds' hopes alive. Rath hit a pitch that broke his bat in two, the heavy end falling on the mound near Cicotte. The ball, however, was hit on the ground to Weaver who threw to Gandil for the out.

The new pitcher for the Reds in the sixth was Adolfo Luque. The Cuban-born Luque was making his second relief appearance in the series. Luque quickly retired the first two White Sox to face him as Ray Schalk flied out to left and Eddie Cicotte, who turned around to hit left handed, struck out. However, Shano Collins then hit the ball past Groh into left field for a double, his third hit of the game. Luque then got Eddie Collins to swing and miss at a third strike. But Ivy Wingo fumbled the ball and had to throw to Daubert at first for the out.

Jake Daubert led off the home half of the sixth and struck out taking the pitch. Heinie Groh followed by driving a Cicotte pitch that cleared the fence in front of the temporary left field bleachers and then rolled under them near the foul line. However, it was ruled a ground-rule double. Edd Roush then tapped the ball back to the mound where Cicotte grabbed and flipped it to Gandil for the out. Groh advanced to third on the play.

The World Series scandal corps speculate that Cicotte could have made a play on Groh at third but elected instead to go to first. This makes no sense whatsoever. With one out and Cicotte having a four-run lead, it was a perfectly normal play to go to first for the second out.

Pat Duncan then drove a clean single through the pitcher's box and Groh trotted home with the Reds' first run of the game.

However, Cicotte brought down the curtain on the Reds rally by getting Larry Kopf to force Duncan at second for the third out.

Luque had no trouble retiring the White Sox in the top of the seventh. Buck Weaver struck out. Joe Jackson hit a grounder to Rath who threw him out at first and Happy Felsch also struck out.

The small partisan crowd in Redland Field came alive and very vocal as the game moved into the bottom of the seventh. Greasy Neale led off and struck out. Eddie Cicotte then walked Ivy Wingo for the third time in the game. Adolpho Luque went up to hit and Cicotte struck him out. However, Morrie Rath followed with a single to keep the Reds' hopes alive. As Jake Daubert came to bat there were cries from the stands for him to hit it out. He then hit the ball hard to Eddie Collins, who knocked it down and threw him out at first, ending the inning.

In the top of the eighth Chick Gandil hit a short fly into left that Larry Kopf went back and hauled in. Swede Risberg followed by hitting the ball into short center. Edd Roush ran in on the ball and dropped it. Risberg rounded first and headed for second, but Roush had recovered in time to throw Risberg out going into the bag. Ray Schalk followed by hitting the ball deep into the hole at short where Larry Kopf made a magnificent stop and threw him out at first.

Eddie Cicotte's shine ball continued to work effectively in the bottom of the eighth as he set the Reds down in order. Heinie Groh flied out to Jackson and both Edd Roush and Pat Duncan grounded out.

Eddie Cicotte led off the top of the ninth for the White Sox and became Luque's fifth strikeout victim. Shano Collins then lined out to Roush and Eddie Collins grounded out, Rath to Daubert. Adolpho Luque had retired the last ten batters in row.

Larry Kopf led off the bottom of the ninth and lined out to Eddie Collins. Greasy Neale flied out to Jackson.

Even with two outs in the bottom of the ninth and the Reds down 4-1, the Reds bench continued to razz the White Sox unmercifully. Suddenly there was life for the hometown team as Ivy Wingo was next up and shot a single into right past Eddie Collins.

Pat Moran then sent Sherry Magee up to hit for Luque. Magee hit a foul back towards the temporary seats in left. Joe Jackson went after the ball and tumbled headfirst over the seat railing attempting an impossible catch. All at once there was silence in the stands as it was thought that Jackson had hurt himself on the attempt to catch Magee's drive. However, after a few seconds Jackson pulled himself up and walked back on the field, and the crowd cheered him wildly.

Magee then singled into right between Gandil and Eddie Collins. Wingo stopped at second. This pinch-hit single was Sherry Magee's first and only World Series hit in a 16-year major league career. Moran, suddenly becoming the strategist, sent in bench jockey Jimmy Smith to run for Magee.

Larry Rath then hit a low liner into right. For some unknown reason Happy Felsch was playing out of position in right rather than center and gathered in Rath's drive down in the right-field corner near the line, ending the game after one hour and forty-seven minutes and sending the series back to Chicago.

For the second day in a row one could chalk up a Reds defeat to poor strategy by manager Pat Moran. In the seventh game he picked the wrong starting pitcher to hang the Reds' World Championship hopes on.

Jim Nasium of the *Philadelphia Inquirer* wrote following the game: "Pat Moran made an unwise choice of pitchers for the seventh game of this hysterical series at Redland Field here this afternoon, and as the White Sox attack which had suddenly revived in the sixth inning of yesterday's game and became vibrant with pulsing life after a period of apathetic idleness resumed today, where it left off yesterday.

"There might have been a different story for us to tell this evening had Moran started the Cuban pitcher, Señor Adolfo Luque, instead of Slim Sallee."[1]

Luque had worked four innings in game seven allowing only one hit and striking out five. He stopped the White Sox cold, but it was just too late to save the game.

The problem with Sallee is that he had a history of Chicago hitting him. Although he had gone the distance in the second game winning 4-2, the White Sox had gotten ten hits off him.

Moran, in selecting Sallee to pitch the seventh game, was counting on containing the White Sox' two best hitters, Joe Jackson and Eddie Collins, who batted left handed. Entering game seven Jackson was having a fine series at the plate hitting .348 (8 for 23). However, Eddie Collins was having a miserable series with the bat, hitting a paltry .091 for the first six games (2 for 22). So Moran's strategy really didn't make much sense at all.

Furthermore, the record clearly showed that Sallee had been hit hard by Joe Jackson, Eddie Collins and Shano Collins in the 1917 World Series. In game one of the 1917 World Series with Sallee pitching for the New York Giants, Shano Collins had gotten three hits off him in the White Sox's 2-1 triumph. In game five of the 1917 series Eddie Collins singled off Sallee in the eighth inning, driving in the go-ahead run and breaking up a 5-5 tie. Overall in the 1917 World Series versus the White Sox, Sallee had a won-lost record of 0-2, giving up 20 hits in 15.1 innings with an ERA of 4.70.

Following the 1918 season in which Sallee achieved an 8-8 record for the Giants, manager John McGraw decided to unload him. The Reds picked up Sallee on waivers from the Giants on March 8, 1919, and of course he then had a remarkable comeback season going 21-7 for the National League Champions.

Ironically, Slim Sallee gave some of the credit for his comeback to a patented cure for his lame back called the "Faradon," distributed by the Frank Richter Service Co. in the Price Hill section of Cincinnati. Sallee stated in advertisements that ran in Cincinnati newspapers, "The Faradon cured me of a lame back, therefore I justly owe my comeback to the marvelous Faradon."[2]

Miracle cures notwithstanding, the fact remains that in game seven of the 1919 World Series versus the White Sox, Sallee gave up nine of the White Sox's ten hits, with Shano Collins, Eddie Collins and Joe Jackson each collecting two hits each before being pulled by Moran after just 4⅓ innings. Furthermore, Shano Collins scored the Sox's first run off Sallee.

Overall, Sallee started four games versus the White Sox in the 1917 and 1919 World Series and pitched a combined total of 28⅔ innings giving up 39 hits while achieving a won-lost record of 1-3.

Pat Moran had six good starting pitchers available for the series. He had gotten away with a win in game two by starting Sallee and should have recognized that stroke of luck and started Adolpho Luque in game seven. Had he done so, despite the rejuvenation of Eddie Cicotte, the series may have been over.

To conclude on the Sallee situation, the *Cincinnati Post* reported following game seven, "When [Joe] Jackson started to mash the ball Wednesday, his first two attempts driving in runs, it was as if he had something on Sallee.

"If Moran is to be criticized then it should be for his selection of pitchers. He is considered to be the best judge of the condition of pitchers in the country, but he must have known that the White Sox were hoping and praying that he would use Sallee."[3]

The rejuvenated Eddie Cicotte, who had started his third game in eight days, pitched a pretty good game for an alleged conspirator. Cicotte went the distance giving up one run and seven hits, just one for extra bases, while striking out four and walking Reds catcher Ivy Wingo three times. Cicotte also got the big out when he needed it as the Reds left a total of nine men on base in the game.

The *Philadelphia Inquirer*, like most newspapers reporting the series around the country, were not blaming Cicotte for the two previous loses he had experienced on the mound in the series, but put the blame where it actually belonged — on the weak bats of his teammates. Following game seven the *Inquirer* reported, "Today's win by the Sox was accomplished through the able pitching of Eddie Cicotte, who had twice tasted defeat and through the batting of his teammates. They staked Cicotte to a run in the first inning and then kept after Slim Sallee, the Reds pitching entry, until they drove him from the mound in the fifth round."[4]

However, it is apparent that the Sox were very determined to return the 1919 World Series to Chicago and if there was a conspiracy taking place then their collective efforts to win in game seven defy logic.

At the end of the seventh game, the National Commission announced that if a ninth game is necessary to decide the series, the Reds had won the coin toss and therefore it would be played in Cincinnati on Friday, October 10.

However, as the Reds arrived back in Chicago for game eight, Heinie Groh was very optimistic about the Reds' chances of wrapping of the series.

"When we left Cincinnati [last night] the Sox had won two straight. That is the most any team had copped in the series. We won two straight twice. We won't do it again. One straight is needed today."[5]

Box Score Game Seven

Chicago	ab	r	h	rbi	Cincinnati	ab	r	h	rbi
S. Collins, rf	5	2	3	0	Rath, 2b	5	0	1	0
E. Collins, 2b	4	1	2	0	Daubert, 1b	4	0	0	0
Weaver, 3b	4	1	0	0	Groh, 3b	4	1	1	0
Jackson, lf	4	0	2	2	Roush, cf	4	0	0	0
Felsch, cf	4	0	2	2	Duncan, lf	4	0	1	1
Gandil, 1b	4	0	0	0	Kopf, ss	4	0	1	0
Risberg, ss	4	0	0	0	Neale, rf	4	0	1	0
Schalk, c	4	0	1	0	Wingo, c	1	0	1	0
Cicotte, p	4	0	0	0	Sallee, p	1	0	0	0
					Fisher, p	0	0	0	0
					Ruether, ph	1	0	0	0
					Luque, p	1	0	0	0
					Magee, ph	1	0	1	0
					Smith, pr	0	0	0	0

Chicago	ip	h	r	er	bb	so
Cicotte	9	7	1	1	3	4

Cincinnati	ip	h	r	er	bb	so
Sallee	4⅓	9	4	2	0	0
Fisher	⅔	0	0	0	0	1
Luque	4	1	0	0	0	5

LOB Chicago 7, Cincinnati 9, E E. Collins, Rath, Daubert, Groh, Roush, 2b S. Collins, Groh, S E. Collins

CHAPTER NINE

Game Eight

At Chicago, October 9, 1919

	1	2	3	4	5	6	7	8	9	R	H	E
Cincinnati	4	1	0	0	1	3	0	1	0	10	16	2
Chicago	0	0	1	0	0	0	0	4	0	5	10	1

Eller
Williams, James (1), Wilkinson (6)

Although the Reds had lost two straight chances at home to wrap up the World Championship, they arrived back in Chicago confident and full of fight for game eight. Also the White Sox fans were still optimistic about the chances of the pale hose crew to take the series despite the Reds' 4-3 advantage.

With the Sox back at home and riding the momentum of a two-game winning streak, the odds in the series established by the betting element were suddenly back in their favor. The *New York Times* reported that the White Sox were favored to win the eighth game of the series today. Odds as high as 6-5 were given in hundreds and 11-10 were the figures in many wagers made this morning at hotels in downtown Chicago.

Also, the *Times* reported that a couple of wealthy lovers of the sport from St. Louis are reported to have placed $5,000 against $9,000 on the series last night backing the Reds.[1]

For game eight, 32,930 fans poured into Comiskey Park. All morning long there had been threatening clouds, which moved over Chicago swiftly. Then as game time approached, the wind was whipping strongly throughout the ballpark. Winds whipped strongly about left and center fields bothering fielders, and whirlwinds of dust were swept two stories high on the base paths.

With the World Championship on the line, White Sox manager Kid Gleason was taking no chances with the treacherous wind. He put his players through a session of high infield fly practice, so that the infielders could get some knowledge of how to handle flies in the wind.

The wind was so strong that at one instance, the fans in the right-field stands were terror stricken when the wind forced the flag pole to sag, leading them to think that the pole would topple on their seats.

Down in the grandstand the Salvation Army sent its ladies into the crowd with tin boxes looking for contributions. However, even the tightly-packed stands suddenly loosened up as the Salvation Army women went through the crowd.[2]

For the Reds, Hod Eller was manager Pat Moran's choice for starting pitcher. Eller had gotten two days rest since his brilliant three-hit shutout in game five.

Lefty Williams would be making his third start of the series for the White Sox. Unsubstantiated rumor has persisted over the past eight decades that prior to game eight Williams' life had been threatened if he won the game. The legend is reported to even have included threats to Williams that he could be shot to death while on the mound. However, there are several versions of the alleged threat and the whole scenario becomes overdramatized in the film *Eight Men Out* when it is portrayed that an agent of perhaps Arnold Rothstein approaches Williams and threatens to murder his wife.

The starting lineups for game eight were the following:

Cincinnati   Chicago

pos.	name	series BA	pos.	name	series BA
2b	Rath	.185	rf	Leibold	.000
1b	Daubert	.200	2b	E. Collins	.144
3b	Groh	.130	3b	Weaver	.310
cf	Roush	.174	lf	Jackson	.370
lf	Duncan	.227	cf	Felsch	.217
ss	Kopf	.208	1b	Gandil	.231

Cincinnati   Chicago

pos.	name	series BA	pos.	name	series BA
rf	Neale	.360	ss	Risberg	.081
c	Rariden	.143	c	Schalk	.263
p	Eller (1-0)	.333	p	Williams (0-2)	.200

When the White Sox took the field for the start of game eight they were greeted with a huge cheer from the fans. However, directly behind the White Sox bench there were two women seated in a box wearing bright crimson turban hats that glistened as the sun came out. It was an ill omen for the team.

Lefty Williams got Reds leadoff batter Morrie Rath to fly out, but that would be the last batter he would retire in his major league career.

Jake Daubert then singled to right field and Heinie Groh did likewise. With two men on the slumping, Edd Roush suddenly came alive with the bat and hit the ball down the first-base line for a double. Daubert scored and Groh held at third. Pat Duncan then hit the ball along the left-field foul line, but Joe Jackson could not get to the ball, permitting both Groh and Roush to score. Duncan was on second with a double.

Larry Kopf stepped into the batter's box and took ball one from Williams. At this point Kid Gleason jumped out of the Sox dugout and headed for the mound to relieve Williams. Gleason brought in "Big Bill" James to relieve Williams, who was making his first appearance in the series.

As Williams walked to the White Sox dugout, one reporter sensing that the end of the series was imminent noted that "Williams had just blown his teammates out of about $2,000 each."[3]

James quickly finished up what Williams had started and walked Larry Kopf. With Duncan on second and Kopf on first, James fanned Greasy Neale for the second out. However, Bill Rariden followed by hitting the ball over Gandil's head for a hit, scoring Duncan with the Reds' fourth run of the inning.

Hod Eller became the ninth Reds batter in the inning, flying out to Felsch.

In the bottom of the first the White Sox wasted no time going after Hod Eller. Nemo Leibold opened up with a line-drive single to left and then Eddie Collins followed with a double to center, Leibold stopping at third.

The White Sox fans cheered wildly, believing that the four-run lead was about to be erased. But suddenly Eller was in control and struck out Buck Weaver. Joe Jackson then hit a long fly down to left that was hauled in by Larry Kopf racing all the way back near the fence. For some unknown reason, Leibold held at third.

Nemo Leibold was not one of the alleged conspirators; therefore, this bonehead base running of his has been historically overlooked. However, had it been Joe Jackson or Chick Gandil that stayed at third on this play, it would have been ballyhooed in movies, books, magazines, etc. for the past 81 years as evidence of cheating by these White Sox players.

Nonetheless, the inning came to an end without the White Sox scoring as Eller fanned Happy Felsch.

Larry Rath led off once again for the Reds in the top of the second, took James to a full count, then struck out. James then got Jake Daubert to line out to Jackson for the second out. Heinie Groh then hit a slow grounder towards Gandil at first. Gandil stayed back on the ball and then it took a bad hop as Groh turned on the hustle to beat it out for an infield hit, his second hit in two innings. Edd Roush then followed with his second hit of the game, continuing to hit the ball to the opposite field with a shot over Jackson's head in left for a double. Groh scored, but Roush, as a result of a quick return throw to the infield by Leibold, was then caught in a run-down between second and third, Leibold to Risberg to Schalk to Weaver to Eddie Collins.

However, the Reds had scored again in the inning, taking a 5-0 lead. More importantly Groh and Roush, their two best hitters who had been slumping throughout the series, had suddenly began to hit and that was bad news indeed for the White Sox.

Chick Gandil led off the Sox's half of the inning and hit the ball to Daubert for an out. Swede Risberg then drew a walk from Eller and Ray Schalk singled to left. However, once again Eller got the job done getting Bill James to foul out to Groh near the Sox bench and then making Nemo Leibold his third strikeout victim of the game.

With a little help from his defense, "Big Bill" James got the Reds out rather efficiently in the top of the third. Pat Duncan grounded out, Weaver to Gandil. Larry Kopf then hit a hard shot towards third that Weaver made a fabulous stop of and threw him out. James then walked Greasy Neale, but Schalk threw him out attempting to steal second.

Eddie Collins led off the bottom of the third for the Sox and lined out to Duncan in left. Buck Weaver followed by hitting a short fly to right that Rath caught on the run.

Joe Jackson then took Eller downtown as he hit a home run high up into the right-field bleachers. This was the only home run hit in the series and one that Jackson would be criticized for hitting immediately after the series and over the ensuing years as an example of his hitting when it didn't count. Also it was evidence to many of his involvement in the alleged conspiracy. There was and still is no mercy in the conspiracy theory for "Shoeless" Joe Jackson. He was simply damned if he hit and damned if he didn't.

A typical report on Jackson's home run was printed in the *Philadelphia Inquirer* following game eight that read in part, "Of course Joe was given a great hand. It was a fine individual effort, but it meant little or nothing towards winning the ball game.

"The game was as good as lost before that mighty swat was made. However it pleased the crowd. The Sox were being beaten, but Sox-less Joe had scored a homer and that was something to be proud of especially with Hod Eller doing the pitching."[4]

Happy Felsch ended the inning by grounding out, Kopf to Daubert.

In the top of the fourth Bill Rariden lined out to Gandil. The Reds then attempted another scoring threat as Bill James hit Hod Eller with a pitch. With Eller on first, Morrie Rath hit a little roller between the box and second. Risberg could not get a hand on it and Rath was on first with a hit, Eller going to second. Next up was Jake Daubert and he stroked a single into center. Eller rounded third attempting to score but was cut down at the plate by a great throw from Leibold. Rath went to third on the play and Daubert took second. However, Heinie Groh ended the scoring threat by flying out to Eddie Collins.

Eller quickly set the Sox down in order in the bottom of the fourth. Chick Gandil flied out to Neale in right. Swede Risberg went down swinging for Eller's fourth strikeout and Ray Schalk grounded out, Groh to Daubert.

Edd Roush led off the Cincinnati fifth and grounded out, Eddie Collins to Gandil. Pat Duncan then lined out to Collins.

However, with two out Larry Kopf came up swinging away on James and hit the ball over the first base bag down the right-field line for a triple. Greasy Neale then followed by hitting the ball toward Weaver at third, but he held back and appeared to let Risberg make the play. However, Risberg seemed confused and the ball went past him into left for a hit, scoring Kopf with the Reds' sixth run of the game. With Bill Rariden up, Neale stole second. However, Rariden then grounded out, Risberg to Gandil.

In what made absolutely no sense at all with the White Sox trailing the Reds 6-1 and the entire Sox pitching corps sitting on the bench, Kid Gleason allowed "Big Bill" James to be his leadoff batter in the bottom of the fifth. During the 1919 season James had played for three American

League teams, Detroit, Boston and Chicago, with a combined batting average of .154. James became Eller's fifth strikeout in the game.

Nemo Leibold followed with a hard smash towards Kopf who made a running stop, then threw to first for the out. Eddie Collins then ended the inning as he too hit the ball hard to Kopf who fielded the ball and threw to Daubert for the out.

Hod Eller led off the sixth for the Reds and hit the ball hard past James. Eddie Collins attempted to get to the ball but could not make a play. James then walked Morrie Rath.

This brought Kid Gleason to the mound and Roy Wilkinson relieved James. Wilkinson was making his second appearance in the series having pitched four innings in relief of Eddie Cicotte in game one.

The first batter to face Wilkinson was Jake Daubert who laid down a bunt in front of the plate. The runners advanced with Eller being safe at third on a wild throw by Schalk to Weaver.

With bases loaded and no outs, Wilkinson struck out Heinie Groh. But his luck ended there as Edd Roush followed with his third hit of the game, bouncing the ball over the head of Eddie Collins. Eller scored, Rath scored, Daubert went to third and Roush playing heads-up ball took second on the play.

The Reds now held an 8-1 lead, but the rally continued as Pat Duncan hit a single into center scoring Daubert and sending Roush to third. The Reds continued to pour on the hustle as Duncan took second on Leibold's throw in an attempt to get Roush at third.

Larry Kopf then walked, loading the bases again. Greasy Neale then forced Roush at the platter for the second out, Weaver to Schalk. Finally the devastating top of the sixth inning came to an end for the White Sox as Schalk caught Kopf off of second with a quick throw to Risberg.

The Reds held a 9-1 lead as the White Sox came up to bat in the bottom of the sixth. Buck Weaver attempted to get something going for the Sox and hit a grounder to Daubert that went for a hit. However, the hopes of the Sox quickly faded as Eller got Joe Jackson to fly out to Roush, likewise for Happy Felsch, and then Chick Gandil flied out to Neale.

As the game entered the top of the seventh, Bill Rariden led for the Reds and hit a fly ball to Felsch in center for an out. Wilkinson then fanned Hod Eller but walked Morrie Rath. Rath then stole second. Jake Daubert also drew a walk from Wilkinson, before Heinie Groh flied out to Leibold in right.

For Groh this was the third time in the game that he failed to deliver a hit with runners in scoring position. In actuality Groh had failed to deliver hits in strategic situations far more times in the series than Joe

Jackson. Yet it is Jackson rather than Groh who is castigated for not delivering hits when they were needed.

Eller entered the bottom of the seventh on cruise control. It just seemed that there was no way to beat him and he quickly retired the Sox in the inning. Swede Risberg flied out to Rath in short center. Ray Schalk fouled out to Rariden and Roy Wilkinson became Eller's sixth strike of the game.

The Reds added another insurance run in the top of the eighth. Wilkinson hit Roush with a pitch and Duncan laid down a sacrifice, Wilkinson to Gandil. Larry Kopf then fouled out to Weaver. The Reds then got a second runner aboard as Wilkinson walked Greasy Neale. With Neale on first and Roush on second, Bill Rariden hit a single into left scoring Roush with the Reds' tenth run. Neale went on to third and Rariden went to second on Jackson's throw to the plate. However, Hod Eller was next up and grounded out to Risberg to end the inning.

As the game moved into the bottom of the eighth with the Reds leading 10-1 it looked hopeless for the White Sox. Nemo Leibold led off and flied out to Neale in right.

A lot of the Sox fans were starting to leave the park but momentarily held their seats when Eddie Collins hit a single into center. Buck Weaver then quickly followed with a double over the head of Daubert, sending Collins to third. Next, Joe Jackson hit the ball into right field scoring Collins and Weaver, then pulled up at second with a double.

Suddenly the Reds' lead had been cut to 10-3, and Joe Jackson, the man that didn't hit in the series when it counted, had driven in all three White Sox runs in the game.

The Sox fans knew that they were facing a long shot but had hope. A long one would cut the lead even further. As Happy Felsch came up to bat, the rejuvenated White Sox crowd was yelling, "Happy, Happy! Smash it into the crowd Happy!" But all Felsch could manage was to lift a little fly ball that was caught by Daubert for the second out.

For a brief moment there was silence in Comiskey Park.

Then the crowd began to hoot and holler again as Chick Gandil came to bat. Gandil hit a long drive to right that Neale appeared to lose in the sun. At first Neale sighted the ball but kept looking the wrong way. Roush, taking notice that Neale had lost sight of the ball, ran it down as the ball rolled to the fence. Jackson scored, Gandil pulled up at third base and the crowd had a good laugh on Neale.

The Sox fans, starting to get hoarse, began to yell for Risberg to do something to keep the rally going. However, Risberg didn't need to do much. The Reds kept the rally going as Swede hit a little fly into center that was misjudged by Roush. Gandil crossed the plate with the fourth Chicago run of the inning.

The rally fell short, however, as Ray Schalk grounded out, Rath to Daubert, ending the inning.

In the Cincinnati ninth Morrie Rath led off by hitting a grounder to Risberg. Even with a 10-5 lead, Rath showed that determined Cincinnati hustle and beat it out for a hit. The hit was the Reds' 16th in the game. Jake Daubert then sacrificed, sending Rath to second. Heinie Groh again failed to hit with a man in scoring position as he flied out to Leibold in right. Edd Roush followed by grounding out, Weaver to Gandil.

Hod Eller took the mound for the bottom of the ninth with the World Championship on the line. Kid Gleason sent Eddie Murphy up to hit for Wilkinson. Eller hit Murphy with a pitch and suddenly there was life again for the Sox.

But Eller then tightened up his grip on the ball. Nemo Leibold hit the ball into center where Roush made a diving catch.

However, Eddie Collins followed with a single, sending Murphy to second. Buck Weaver then hit a fly ball to right caught by Neale. Murphy took third on the play. Joe Jackson came up to bat with two runners on and two outs. Eddie Collins then stole second base. But Eller gets Jackson to ground out, Rath to Daubert, ending the series.

As Jake Daubert gloved the final out there was no player pile-on at the mound or players charging out of the dugout as is commonly done today at the climactic moment of the World Series. In 1919 the World Champion Cincinnati Reds simply walked off the field with their heads held high.

As the crowd was leaving Comiskey Park, none of the remarks that were overheard were against the White Sox. They all seemed to be in favor of the Reds. The Chicago fans were a sophisticated baseball community and most seemed to agree that Cincinnati winning the world's title for the first time was a good thing for baseball. In the lingo of today, they had been there and done that. They were aware it took a very good baseball team in the Reds to so handily beat the White Sox.

Back in Cincinnati as soon as the ticker tapes in taverns, banks and newspapers made the final score of the 10-5 Reds' triumph official, children began running up and down neighborhood streets yelling out the news. Soon throngs of adults joined in the celebration, yelling out of windows from the Walnut Hills to the "Over the Rein" district to Price Hill.

Reds manager Pat Moran told the *New York Times*, "The Reds are champions and I'm the happiest man in the world tonight. I cannot praise my players highly enough. They played a remarkable ball game,

Pat Moran and Kid Gleason, White Sox, 1919 World Series, Chicago. (Chicago Historical Society, ICHI-31480. Photography: *Chicago Daily News.*)

fought every minute to win and there was never a time when they lost confidence.

"Eller got himself in a couple of holes today, but he recovered quickly and had the Sox at his mercy. I want to say that the Sox are not quitters. They are a game lot of players. They fought to win, but were outclassed in my opinion."[5]

White Sox skipper Kid Gleason was brief in his postgame remarks. "If Williams had shown some stuff in the first inning, it would have been a different story to tell tonight. That first inning when the Reds scored four runs was enough to take the heart out of any ball club."[6]

But if Kid Gleason had Urban "Red" Faber available to pitch game eight against Eller it just might have been a different story. Assuming Faber would have beaten the Reds, then Gleason would have had Dickie Kerr available to pitch game nine against either Dutch Ruether or Jimmy Ring.

Having a ninth game in the 1919 World Series would have been one of the most exciting contests in the history of the series. But playing a ninth game, regardless of which team won, would not have historically defused the controversy of an alleged conspiracy. Notwithstanding sportswriter Hugh Fullerton, there were a lot of reputations on the line with the pre-series hype on the superiority myth of the White Sox, and even if the Reds had lost the series in nine games, there are those who would still be arguing until this very day that the series was protracted because of the scandal.

The *Philadelphia Inquirer* reported following game eight, "The Red team of Cincinnati walked off the field in dignified triumph. Had the Sox won the game there would have been a wonderful demonstration. But the best ball team had won the game and series— at least the team that played better ball and won deservingly."[7]

Box Score Game Eight

Cincinnati	ab	r	h	rbi	Chicago	ab	r	h	rbi
Rath, 2b	4	1	2	0	Leibold, rf	5	0	1	0
Daubert, 1b	4	2	2	0	E. Collins, 2b	5	1	3	0
Groh, 3b	6	2	2	0	Weaver, 3b	5	1	2	0
Roush, cf	5	2	3	4	Jackson, lf	5	2	2	3
Duncan, lf	4	1	2	3	Felsch, cf	4	0	0	0
Kopf, ss	3	1	1	0	Gandil, 1b	4	1	1	1
Neale, rf	3	0	1	1	Risberg, ss	3	0	0	1
Rariden, c	5	0	2	2	Schalk, c	4	0	1	0
Eller, p	4	1	1	0	Williams, p	0	0	0	0
					James, p	2	0	0	0
					Wilkinson, p	1	0	0	0
					Murphy, ph	0	0	0	0

Cincinnati	ip	h	r	er	bb	so
Eller	9	10	5	4	1	6

Chicago						
Williams	⅓	4	4	4	0	0
James	4⅔	8	4	3	3	2
Wilkinson	4	4	2	0	4	2

LOB Cincinnati 12, Chicago 8, E Roush, Rariden, Schalk, 2b Roush (2), E. Collins, Weaver, Jackson, Duncan, 3b Kopf, Gandil, HR Jackson, S Daubert, Duncan, SB Rath, Neale, Rariden, E. Collins, HBP James, Wilkinson, Eller

CHAPTER TEN

World Champions

On Friday, October 10, 1919, the Reds arrived home in Cincinnati as World Champions. Mayor John Galvin declared a half-holiday in the city. Superintendent Randall J. Condon ordered all public schools closed. Many of the parochial school children in the city were also given a holiday to join in the celebration.

As St. Joseph's College played victory marches leading a procession to Fountain Square, the *Cincinnati Post* reported,

"The World Champion Reds came home Friday and were marched up town like presidents and kings."[1]

"Thru a double line of cheering men and smiling stenographers and saleswomen just going to work the conquerors made triumphal entry."

"All that was lacking to make it a Roman holiday were the prostrate forms of the White Sox dragging at the wheels of our heroes' chariots."

"Thousands also crowded Fountain Square to feast their eyes on the conquerors and shake them by the hand, for it had been announced that at 10 o'clock they would be there to be seen by all."

The eight-game series had been a huge financial success as well. Official paid attendance was 236,928. Official receipts (excluding tax) were $722,414. The loss of the series had to be softened somewhat for White Sox owner Charles Comiskey when he received a check for the Chicago club share of $87,156.47. Of course as this purse is split right down the middle for the ball clubs, the Cincinnati Reds owners were presented a likewise amount through August Gary Herrmann.

The Reds winning players' share was $117,157.35. The money was distributed that afternoon in the Reds offices in the Wiggins Block building. The *Cincinnati Post* on October 10, 1919, ran a large photo on its front page of Reds Captain Heinie Groh receiving the check from John E. Bruce of the National Commission, drawn on The Fifth-Third National Bank of Cincinnati for the players, with Jake Daubert, Morrie Rath and manager Pat Moran standing by him.

Each of the twenty regulars on the Reds along with manager Pat Moran received a check for $5,207.01. Pat Duncan, who had joined the team late in the season from the Southern League and played in just 31 regular-season games, received $2,612.67. Others receiving various shares included trainer Doc Hoskins, $2,612.66; Hank Schreiber, $500 (played 19 games in the infield); Charley See, $300 (played 8 games in the outfield), business manager Frank C. Bancroft, $1,000; groundskeeper Matty Schawb, $250; press gate tender Lou Wolfson, $100; and the clubhouse boy, $50.[2]

The total Chicago player's share was $78,104.90, approximately $3,254.36 for each player. Of course there were a few White Sox that also received some additional cash payments from unnamed sources.

1919 World Series — Final Team Totals and Player Statistics

Team Totals

	W	AB	H	2B	3B	HR	R	RBI	BA	BB	SO	ERA
CIN	5	251	64	10	7	0	35	33	.255	25	22	1.63
CHI	3	263	59	10	3	1	20	17	.224	15	30	3.68

Individual Batting: Cincinnati

Player	BA	AB	Hits	2B	3B	HR	R	RBI
D. Ruether-P	.667	6	4	1	2	0	2	4
I. Wingo-C	.571	7	4	0	0	0	1	1
S. Magee-PH	.500	2	1	0	0	0	0	0
R. Fisher-P	.500	2	1	0	0	0	0	0
G. Neale-OF	.357	28	10	1	1	0	3	4
H. Eller-P	.286	7	2	1	0	0	2	0
P. Duncan-OF	.269	26	7	2	0	0	3	8
J. Daubert-1B	.241	29	7	0	1	0	4	1

Player	BA	AB	Hits	2B	3B	HR	R	RBI
M. Rath-2B	.226	31	7	1	0	0	5	2
L. Kopf-SS	.222	27	6	0	2	0	3	2
E. Roush-CF	.214	28	6	2	1	0	6	7
B. Rariden-C	.211	19	4	0	0	0	0	2
H. Groh-3B	.172	29	5	2	0	0	6	2
D. Luque-P	.000	1	0	0	0	0	0	0
J. Ring-P	.000	5	0	0	0	0	0	0
S. Sallee-P	.000	4	0	0	0	0	0	0
J. Smith-PR	—	0	0	0	0	0	0	0

Individual Batting: Chicago

Player	BA	AB	Hits	2B	3B	HR	R	RBI
F. McMullin-PH	.500	2	1	0	0	0	0	0
J. Jackson-OF	.375	32	12	3	0	1	5	6
B. Weaver-3B	.324	34	11	4	1	0	4	0
R. Schalk-C	.304	23	7	0	0	0	1	2
S. Collins-OF	.250	16	4	1	0	0	2	0
C. Gandil-1B	.233	30	7	0	1	0	1	5
E. Collins-2B	.226	31	7	1	0	0	2	1
L. Williams-P	.200	5	1	0	0	0	0	0
H. Felsch-OF	.192	26	5	1	0	0	2	3
D. Kerr-P	.167	6	1	0	0	0	0	0
S. Risberg-SS	.080	25	2	0	1	0	3	0
N. Leibold-OF	.056	18	1	0	0	0	0	0
E. Cicotte-P	.000	8	0	0	0	0	0	0
B. James-P	.000	2	0	0	0	0	0	0
G. Lowdermilk-P	.000	1	0	0	0	0	0	0
B. Lynn-C	.000	1	0	0	0	0	0	0
E. Mayer-P	.000	1	0	0	0	0	0	0
E. Murphy-PH	.000	2	0	0	0	0	0	0
R. Wilkinson-P	.000	2	0	0	0	0	0	0

Individual Stolen Bases

Cincinnati	Chicago
M. Rath 2	E. Collins
E. Roush 2	C. Gandil
J. Daubert 2	S. Risberg
H. Groh 2	N. Leibold
L. Kopf	R. Schalk
R. Fisher	
G. Neale	
B. Rariden	

Individual Errors

Cincinnati	Chicago
M. Rath-2	S. Risberg-4
E. Roush-2	E. Cicotte-2
J. Daubert-2	E. Collins-2
H. Groh-2	H. Felsch-2
L. Kopf	C. Gandil
R. Fisher	R. Schalk
G. Neale	
B. Rariden	

Individual Pitching

Cincinnati

Pitcher	W	L	ERA	IP	H	BB	SO	SV
H. Eller	2	0	2.00	18	13	2	15	0
J. Ring	1	1	0.64	14	7	6	4	0
D. Ruether	1	0	2.57	14	12	4	1	0
S. Sallee	1	1	1.35	13.1	19	1	2	0
R. Fisher	0	1	2.35	7.2	7	2	2	0
D. Luque	0	0	0.00	5	1	0	0	0

Chicago

Pitcher	W	L	ERA	IP	H	BB	SO	SV
E. Cicotte	1	2	2.91	21.2	19	5	7	0
D. Kerr	2	0	1.42	19	14	3	6	0
L. Williams	0	3	6.61	16.1	12	8	4	0
R. Wilkinson	0	0	3.68	7.1	9	4	3	0
B. James	0	0	5.79	4.2	8	3	2	0
G. Loudermilk	0	0	9.00	1	2	1	0	0
E. Mayer	0	0	0.00	1	0	1	0	0

CHAPTER ELEVEN

September 1920

All the celebrating over the World Championship in Cincinnati came to an end. For most sports fans the 1919 World Series soon faded in their memories like the falling leaves of late autumn and suddenly there was the smell of college football in the air. Nonetheless, subtle talk of games having been fixed in the World Series simmered over the next ten months.

Charles A. Comiskey, owner of the Chicago White Sox, even began a private investigation and called John A. Heydler, president of the National League, and told him that he suspected some of his White Sox players in fixing games. Furthermore, Comiskey stated that he, along with Chicago Cubs President William Veeck, had obtained a confession from Lee Magee in regards to a game he attempted to throw in 1918.

Then spring arrived and the 1920 baseball season began. The 1920 season like the year before was highly successful at the gate with a record 9.1 million fans going through the turnstiles. However, in late September the story broke in the press of a possible conspiracy by eight Chicago White Sox players to throw the 1919 World Series.

The whole affair boiled over in September 1920 when news broke in the press about an alleged collaboration between gambling elements and some of the Chicago White Sox players to throw games in the 1919 World Series. At that time the grand jury had been seated in Chicago to hear evidence in regard to gambling influences on baseball and their investigation quickly led to several White Sox players in the 1919 World Series.

I mention these events not in the name of fairness in my argument but rather accuracy. As any seasoned politician can tell you, fairness and accuracy bear no relationship in cause and effect. While it is certainly not necessary for me to chronicle these events to support my argument that the best team won, I strongly believe omitting it would leave a distinguishable void in the historical account and analysis of the controversy surrounding the 1919 World Series and its lasting aftermath. Therefore, I present my analysis as to why I have reached the conclusion that these events are not relevant to the outcome of the series in the next chapter.

Regardless of the news that broke in September 1920 suggesting that baseball had a dark side and that would leave a sour taste in the mouths of fans and owners alike, the 1920 season was still a most exciting and profitable one. The New York Yankees packed in 1,290,000 fans, doubling what they had drawn in 1919 thanks to the colossal blunder of Red Sox owner Harry Frazee. On January 3, 1920, Frazee made the worst deal in baseball history when he sold Babe Ruth to the Yankees for $125,000 and a personal loan of $300,000 so he could finance his stage production of *No, No, Nanette*.

In the National League the St. Louis Cardinals' Rogers Hornsby would hit .370 and win the first of his seven batting titles. Now pitching for the Chicago Cubs, the great Grover Cleveland Alexander, who everyone thought was on a down slide in his career since returning from World War I, would have a terrific comeback season with a league leading won-lost record of (27-14) and ERA of 1.91.

Over in the American League, George Sisler of the St. Louis Browns would hit .407 while winning the batting crown and Babe Ruth, now playing for the New York Yankees, would set a new record for the most home runs in a season by belting 54 round-trippers. Jim Bagby, pitching for the Cleveland Indians, would finish the campaign with a 31-12 record.

The Cincinnati Reds entered the 1920 season fighting hard to defend their World Championship. Most of the season saw the Reds in a tight two-way race with the Brooklyn Robins (Dodgers). However, the race became a three-way contest in August when the New York Giants suddenly surged out of the second division. In September both the Reds and Giants began to falter while Brooklyn continued to forge ahead. Subsequently, following Labor Day the Robins (Dodgers) went on a tear, winning 16 games and losing 2, which spelled disaster for the Reds.

The Reds continued to battle for the pennant through mid-September, and as the end neared they played with a vengeance in a do-or-die slugfest with the New York Giants at the Polo Grounds on Sunday, September 19, 1920.

With every seat in the Polo Grounds sold and thousands of fans still looking for a way into the park, the Reds lost a tough extra-inning game to the Giants 7-6. In the top of the ninth they had victory within their grasp with one out and runners on second and third, when Heinie Groh hit a vicious line drive that was turned into a double play by Giants first baseman George Kelly. Then the game was lost in the bottom of the 11th inning when Pat Duncan fumbled a ball hit to left field by back-up catcher Frank Snyder. The Reds had scored all of their six runs in the game as a result of home runs with men on by Edd Roush, Greasy Neale and relief pitcher Fritz Coumbe.

Meanwhile over in Brooklyn the Robins had defeated the Pirates 4-3 in the bottom of the ninth inning when Bernie Neis doubled, stole third and scored the winning run on a wild throw by Pirates pitcher Wilbur Cooper.

With two weeks to go in the season the chances of the Reds repeating as National League Champions looked bleak indeed. The Robins needed only to win six out of their remaining eight games to clinch the pennant. The second place Giants were trailing Brooklyn by 5 games with 12 games left to play and the third place Reds still had 15 games to play.

John McGraw, sensing that the Giants were not going to catch Brooklyn in the National League pennant race, began making plans to play an exhibition series following the season with the New York Yankees at the Polo Grounds. The National Commission gave its blessing to the exhibition series if it would be scheduled to not conflict with any World Series games being played in Brooklyn.

Therefore it was decided that if Brooklyn and Cleveland or the White Sox should open the series at Ebbets Field on October 5 and play there again on October 6, they would travel west on October 7 for the next two games on October 8 and 9 and come back on October 10. The Giants and Yankees therefore could meet at New York four times while the pennant winning teams were out of town, and then remain idle during their return to Brooklyn.

For the Cincinnati Reds the end to the 1920 National League pennant race came in Pittsburgh on Wednesday, September 22, when they lost a double-header to the Pirates 2-0 and 3-1. That same day a grand jury seated in Chicago began hearing evidence of an alleged conspiracy in a Cubs-Phillies game played on August 31, 1920. Almost immediately the focus of the hearing turned to the 1919 World Series. Now the never-ending humiliation of the 1919 Reds team would begin.

The second place Giants would be knocked out of the pennant race on September 27 when they lost the second game of a double-header to the Boston Braves 3-2 as Braves third baseman Tony Boeckel hit a home run in the top of the ninth off Giant starter Rosy Ryan. Ryan was making his one and only start of the 1920 campaign in this crucial game. The Giants would finish in second place seven games off the mark.

The Reds concluded the 1920 season finishing third, 10½ games behind Brooklyn. Nonetheless, the Reds continued to be solid at the plate in 1920. They had a team batting average of .277, equal to that of the pennant winning Brooklyn club. Edd Roush finished third in hitting in the National League with an average of .339, while Jake Daubert hit .304, Heinie Groh.298 and Pat Duncan .295.

But their pitching, which had been so brilliant in handicapping the Chicago White Sox hitters in the 1919 World Series, suddenly slumped in 1920. Jimmy Ring went 17-16, Dutch Ruether 16-12, and Dolf Luque 13-9, each having reasonably good seasons. But Hod Eller (13-12), Ray Fisher (10-11) and Slim Sallee (5-6) were nowhere as effective as they had been in the 1919 season and were hardly effective at all coming down the stretch in September. In fact the Reds became so disenchanted with Sallee that on September 5, 1920, they sent him packing on waivers to the New York Giants.

However, in fairness to Eller, the major leagues rules committee had made some radical changes in the playing rules prior to the 1920 season that included outlawing his meat and potatoes pitch, the shine ball. Essentially the rules change stated that beginning in the 1920 season the spitball and other unorthodox deliveries were abolished. While special provisions were made to allow each team to name two pitchers as spitball pitchers for the 1920 season, thereafter no spitballers were to be allowed. Eller's shine ball, however, came under the category of unorthodox deliveries.

Final National League Standings 1920

Team	Won	Lost	PCT	GB
Brooklyn	93	61	.604	
New York	86	68	.558	7
Cincinnati	82	71	.536	10½
Pittsburgh	79	75	.513	14
Chicago	75	79	.487	18
St. Louis	75	79	.487	18
Boston	62	90	.408	30
Philadelphia	62	91	.405	30½

Some suggest that if the Cincinnati Reds would have repeated as

National League Champions in 1920, then it would have legitimized their 1919 World Series victory. How absolutely disingenuous and absurd this logic is.

The Pittsburgh Pirates won the 1960 World Series over the powerful New York Yankees despite being both outhit 91-60 and outscored 55-27. But I have yet to hear someone suggest that if the Pittsburgh Pirates would have repeated as National League Champions in 1961 following their fluke win over the Yankees in the 1960 World Series then it would have legitimized their World Championship.

The White Sox were in fact a stronger team than the 1919 club and featured four 20-game winning pitchers. The 1920 Sox mound corps were led by a recuperated Urban Red Faber (23-13), along with Eddie Cicotte (21-10), Lefty Williams (22-14) and Dickie Kerr (21-9). In the American League batting title race, Joe Jackson wound up in third place with an average of .382 while Eddie Collins finished fifth with an average of .369. Happy Felsch also had a big year, hitting .338 with 14 home runs and 115 RBIs.

The Chicago White Sox were also locked in a heated three-team pennant race in 1920 with the Cleveland Indians and New York Yankees. In late August the White Sox were holding down first place with rumors beginning to circulate of unscrupulous play by the team in the 1919 World Series. Then the Sox went into a tailspin and lost six straight games just prior to Labor Day, wiping out a meager 3½ lead over the Indians.

Eddie Collins went to see White Sox Owner Charles Comiskey following the tailspin in late August and told Chommy that it was his opinion that the Sox had dumped a critical three game series with Boston.

On Sunday, September 19, the Indians' Jim Bagby won his 29th game of the season, pitching a 2-0 shutout over the Boston Red Sox to keep the Tribe out in front of the White Sox by three games in the American League pennant race. The Indians now needed to win only 7 of their remaining 13 games to wrap up the American League flag.

A grand jury in Chicago had been investigating reports that a game between the Chicago Cubs and Philadelphia Phillies played on August 31 had been fixed. However, on Wednesday, September 22, 1920, the grand jury suddenly changed its focus and began hearing testimony about an alleged fix in the 1919 World Series.

Hartley Replogle, prosecutor in charge of the grand jury probe into the alleged scandal in the 1919 World Series, issued a statement in regards to the day's proceedings. "Seven Chicago players are involved, but none of the Cincinnati players were implicated." He also mentioned that several witnesses were not living up to their pledges that they would make public all the information that they had.[1]

Those persons questioned on September 22 included Ban Johnson, president of the American League, and Presidents Charles Comiskey of the Chicago White Sox and William Veeck of the Chicago Cubs, as well as several baseball writers.

Following his appearance before the grand jury, Ban Johnson told reporters he had presented testimony which he believed proved some players had thrown games last year, but he had no evidence of such actions this year.

William Veeck had presented to the grand jury a stack of reports written by private detectives. The reports were in reference to charges that the Philadelphia Phillies versus Chicago Cubs game on August 31 had been fixed for the Phillies to win. However, Veeck was adamant in stating that none of the reports provided to the grand jury contained any conclusive proof against players on the Chicago Cubs being involved in any game fixing.

Other witnesses that testified in the first day's hearing included baseball writers Sam Hall and I. E. Sanborn. They were questioned mainly in regard to their opinions on how many players on a team would have to be in on a fix to ensure a victory for the other club. Hall stated that he believed that two men could assure a defeat for their team under ordinary circumstances. Also the two were questioned concerning their knowledge of betting in baseball.

Rube Benton, a pitcher for the New York Giants, was expected to testify the next day and John Heydler, president of the National League, was scheduled to be examined on next Monday or Tuesday.

Subpoenas were issued following the first day's hearings for John J. McGraw, manager of the New York Giants, and Barry McCormick, an umpire in the Chicago versus Philadelphia game of August 31. Also subpoenas were issued to John Seys, secretary of the Chicago Cubs; Ray Schalk, catcher for the Chicago White Sox; and William Birch, a former newspaperman. They were ordered to appear on the following Tuesday.

Prosecutor Replogle also stated that Charles Stoneham, president of the New York Giants, and Joe Villa, a well-known newspaperman, would be asked to appear later.

By the next day news of the grand jury hearing was in every newspaper in the country. In Cleveland that day as the White Sox and Indians were engaged in hand-to-hand combat for the American League pennant, Joe Jackson rounded the bases after hitting a home run and was jeered by the crowd. Jackson simply responded by raising his middle finger.[2]

In Chicago on September 23, New York Giant pitcher Rube Benton testified at the grand jury probe and implicated four White Sox players in an alleged fix in the 1919 World Series. The entire focus of the probe would now shift to the 1919 World Series.

Grand jury testimony is traditionally sealed, confidential and not made before the public. However, the veil of secrecy was lifted in these proceedings to give baseball the benefit of the doubt with the fans and public at large. Consequently, Rube Benton's testimony before the grand jury in Cook County was immediately printed in scores of newspapers throughout the country.

Benton told the grand jury that Buck Herzog, Hal Chase and Heinie Zimmerman had offered him a bribe to lose a game. In a separate statement Benton named four White Sox players as having been named to him by an alleged member of a gambling ring in a discussion of alleged fixing of the 1919 World Series.

Benton named Eddie Cicotte, pitcher of the first game; Claude Williams, pitcher of the second game; Chick Gandil, first basemen, and Happy Felsch, center fielder. According to Benton's statement, the players were mentioned by a Cincinnati betting commissioner named Hahn.[3]

Benton said that Hahn told him five White Sox players demanded $100,000 for throwing the series and that this was paid to them by a group of Pittsburgh gamblers.

Benton also said in the alleged fixing of the World Series last fall:

> Last fall after the series a man named Hahn who hails from Cincinnati and is known as the betting commissioner, visited me at my home in Clinton, South Carolina. One morning while we were out hunting I asked him about the World Series. He said the series was not on the square.
>
> He said the deal to fix players to throw the series to Cincinnati had been engineered by a syndicate of gamblers from Pittsburgh for whom he worked in Cincinnati as betting commissioner.
>
> He said certain players on the White Sox team had visited Pittsburgh before the series was played and made arrangements to throw the games for a price. He said that the players demanded $100,000 to lay down so that the Sox would lose and this was paid them.
>
> We discussed various players on the team. Buck Weaver's name was not mentioned, nor were the names of Jackson, Eddie Collins, John (Shano) Collins or Ray Schalk. Five players were mentioned by Hahn in the course of the conversation.
>
> The four are Eddie Cicotte, Claude Williams, Chick Gandil and Hap Felsch. Comiskey held up their checks calling for the player's share of the world's series money for some time. I do not recall the name of the fifth man.
>
> I do know the tip was sent out of Cincinnati to bet on the Reds. Jean Dubue, who was a member of the Giants at the time, received a wire instructing him

to bet his bankroll on the Reds. I was in his room at the Ansonia Hotel in New York when he opened the telegram. I was sitting next to him and read the message. I do not remember who signed it.

They tell me around New York that Hal Chase won $40,000 on the series. He must have won a lot because he had plenty of money after the series ended. I understand his and Dubue's information came from the same man.

I made one small wager on the series. I bet $20 on the first game and won it. I spent it for drinks in the barroom where I made the wager. I did not even touch the money.

After the first bet, Larry Doyle [second baseman, 1920 Giants] and I made a piker bet on every game. Doyle liked the White Sox and bet on them. I had my "tip" and liked the Reds. But my winnings were very small, only $10 or $20 a day.[4]

Whether Benton perjured himself in front of the grand jury is not known. However, allegedly two unnamed Chicago Cubs players had told the same grand jury that Benton had remarked to them that he had won $8,000 betting on the Cincinnati Reds in the 1919 World Series.

As the grand jury concluded its session for the day, it was announced that they planned to recall American League president Ban Johnson sometime in the next week. Other possible witnesses to be called included National League president John Heydler and possibly Broadway theatrical producer George M. Cohan and Monty Tennes of Chicago. Cohan was reported to have lost $30,000 on the 1919 World Series and Tennes $80,000.

Following Benton's testimony to the grand jury that leaked out to the press, White Sox President Charles Comiskey offered the following statement that was published the next day on September 24, 1920.

It was nearly nine months ago that Mr. Johnson [Ban] who is president of our league [American], gave out interviews referring to gambling in connection with baseball. Immediately afterwards the Board of Directors of the American League called upon Mr. Johnson for proof to substantiate his statements so that the board might eradicate the evil, but Johnson did not even attend the meeting of the board, much less give the desired information.

The World Series of 1919 started on the third of October, 1919, in Cincinnati. Immediately I began to hear rumors that some of my ball players had been fixed. I sent for John Heydler, the president of the National League and a member of the National Commission. This was the morning of the second game. I told him of the rumors I had heard. I told Mr. Heydler that I was sending for him and not Mr. Johnson because I had no confidence in Johnson.

I immediately sent for manager Gleason. I also told him of these same rumors. I told Gleason to take out any ball player who did not appear to be doing his best. The stories of "fixing" would not go down. I offered a reward of $10,000 for proof of the fixing of any of my ball players. I head that a gambler in East St. Louis had been crossed by the gamblers and had lost $5,500 on the game, that he would tell the story of the alleged frame-up if he could get his $5,500 back.

I sent manager Gleason and another man to East St. Louis and offered to pay this man the $5,500 in question if he would give us this information, but to no avail.

I employed a large force of detectives to run down every clue and paid them more than $4,000 for their services in running down every clue imaginable but could get nothing tangible.

After the World Series, I withheld for several weeks the World's Series checks of my ball players whose names had been rightfully or wrongfully mentioned in connection with the scandal and it was only after I could get no evidence of crookedness that I thereby sent the checks in question to the players on my club.

At no time since the players of the World's Series did I have any cooperation from Johnson or any member of the National Commission in ferreting out this charge of crookedness.

Johnson now says that an official investigation was made — if so it was made unknown to me, my manager or my ball players. The results of such an alleged investigation have never been communicated to me or to the league.

In line with the policy I have always pursued, I have offered to the State's attorney of Cook County and the judge of the criminal court who has charge of the present grand jury every assistance by way of money or otherwise to turn up any evidence of crookedness that exists affecting the honesty or integrity of this great American pastime — baseball.

I'll go further; if any of my players are not honest, I'll fire them, no matter who they are; and if I can't get honest players to fill their places I'll close the games at the park that I spent a lifetime to build and which in the declining years of my life I take the greatest measure of pride and pleasure.[5]

Chicago manager Kid Gleason, contacted in Cleveland where the Sox were playing a crucial series, had the following to say about the grand jury probe: "We are trying our best to win the pennant this year, all reports to the contrary. I have nothing further to say."[6]

The White Sox players scoffed at the report and pointed to their overwhelming victory over Cleveland yesterday as evidence of their determination to win. They said no player of the team was implicated in any gambling syndicate.

In Cincinnati the man named Hahn mentioned in the testimony of Rube Benton as the one who told him that the 1919 World Series was fixed could not be located. It could have been that Hahn had left town or that he simply did not exist at all.

National League president John Heydler was in Detroit investigating rumors in connection with the betting on the August 31 game between the Chicago Cubs and Philadelphia Phillies, where he made the following statement in regard to the day's grand jury proceedings.

> Every championship game played in the National League in 1919 as well as this season has been won or lost strictly on its merits. I challenge any of these muck-rakers either inside or outside the ranks of professional baseball to appear before the Chicago grand jury and prove otherwise.
>
> Regardless of the alleged attempted "fixing" of the first two games of the last World's Series, I always have contended and do now contend, that the best team won the pennant on the level.
>
> If the testimony given by pitcher Benton of our New York club is correctly set forth in today's press accounts, then that fellow either perjured himself before the grand jury or in his private examination before me.[7]

On the evening of September 25, Harry H. Brigham, foreman of the Cook County grand jury listening to testimony in the conspiracy probe, told newspaper reporters that the name of the man who "fixed" the 1919 World Series for Cincinnati to win had been given to the grand jury. This man, Brigham stated, acted as a representative of a ring of gamblers who offered Chicago White Sox players money to throw games. That man's name according to Brigham was Arnold Rothstein of New York, a millionaire turfman and owner of de Grace racetrack.[8]

Others implicated according to Brigham were former major league pitcher William Burns and Abe Attell, former featherweight boxing champion, along with several other well-known sportsmen.

As the American League pennant race entered the final week of the 1920 season, the Cleveland Indians and Chicago White Sox were locked in an air-tight race only separated by one game for the lead. On Sunday, September 26, the White Sox had an easy time defeating Detroit 8-1 behind the pitching of Eddie Cicotte, who won his 21st game of the season with the tide of suspicion rolling in on him. This would be the last game ever pitched by Eddie Cicotte in his major league career.

The following day, Monday, September 27, the American League pennant race remained nearly deadlocked. Out in St. Louis the league leading Indians defeated the Browns 8-4. In the game George Sisler, leading the league with a batting average of .408, got three hits to tie the American League season mark of 248 set by Ty Cobb in 1911.

In Chicago the White Sox kept up the pace behind the six-hit pitching of Dickie Kerr as he shut out the Tigers 2-0. The White Sox scored all their runs in the bottom of the sixth inning when Tiger pitcher Hooks

Dauss hit Buck Weaver with a pitch, then gave up back to back singles to Eddie Collins and Joe Jackson, followed by a poor throw to the plate from Ty Cobb in center field. The game was the last one scheduled at Comiskey Park for the 1920 season and the victory for the Sox was their tenth in the last 11 games as Joe Jackson hitting .384 and Eddie Collins .367 were leading a blistering attack.

With just six games left for the Indians to play and three for the White Sox, the standings in the American League pennant race on the morning of Tuesday, September 28, 1920, were the following.

American League Standings

Team	Won	Lost	Pct.
Cleveland	94	54	.635
Chicago	95	56	.629
New York	93	59	.612
St. Louis	74	74	.500
Boston	71	80	.470
Washington	64	82	.438
Detroit	59	91	.393
Philadelphia	47	101	.318

While the controversy grew from the grand jury probe, plans were well in progress for the 1920 World Series. In Chicago the National Commission met and had a coin toss for the setting of the home games in the series. The American League won the toss and subsequently the first game was set to be played in either Cleveland or Chicago on October 5. As the memory of the increased revenues from the 1919 World Series was still fresh in their minds, the Commission decided to again play a nine-game series in 1920. The game sequence was changed though, having the first three played in the American League city and the next four in the National League city. Subsequently, if the eighth game was necessary, it would be played in the American League city and the ninth in the National League city.

The Commission also decided that if it were necessary to break a tie for the American League Championship, then a three-game series would be played. The first game would be played in Cleveland, the second in Chicago and the third, if necessary, on neutral grounds. Therefore, if a tie necessitated the start of the World Series, it would be delayed accordingly.

The National Commission concluded its meeting with the acknowledgment that for the first time in fifteen years the familiar face of Commission Chairman, Cincinnati Reds president August Gary Herrmann, who had resigned from the commission last fall, was missing. Commission secretary John E. Bruce acted as chairman in the absence of Herrmann.

Herrmann had recently been subpoenaed by the grand jury and was expected to testify at 10:00 A.M. on October 1. He wasn't sure how relevant his testimony would be however. "I heard a world of rumors and gossip," Herrmann said. "Of course I am intensely interested in the present investigation as bearing so directly on the series won by our ball club last fall. I have never had much information on the doings of the American League players. My testimony therefore may not be of as much assistance in the present case. But I'll help all I can."[9]

In Cleveland, Indians management was confident that the 1920 World Series was imminent and work was beginning on constructing temporary stands to hold an additional 6,500 seats at League Park. The stands were to be constructed over Lexington Avenue at a cost of about $15,000 and would increase the capacity of the ballpark to 27,000 for the series.

James C. Dunn, president of the Indians, was quoted as saying, "It's a gamble with me. But inasmuch as the stands could be completed in less than seven days. I could not afford to wait until the winner of the flag is declared."[10]

However, Dunn was leaving immediately for Chicago in order to request that the National Commission delay the start of the World Series until October 7 to allow him time to finish constructing the extra stands.

That evening in the September 27 edition of the *Philadelphia North American* Billy Maharg told his story of the scandal. Maharg issued a statement connecting Eddie Cicotte with the alleged gambling plot and charging that Abe Attell had headed up the gambling ring. He further asserted that the White Sox players were double-crossed by Attell and never received the $100,000 sum said to have been promised to them. Maharg asserted that it was late in the series before they learned this. Attell kept postponing the day of settlement, saying he needed the money to bet. As a result of Attell reneging on the payoff, the players fought back against the gamblers by winning a game they were supposed to lose.

As arrangements for the grand jury to reconvene on September 28 were being made, American League President Ban Johnson had heard rumors that gamblers were creating an impression that the Chicago White Sox do not dare win the 1920 American League pennant. Chicago newspapers were reporting that Johnson had said that a syndicate of gamblers that bought last year's World Series by paying $100,000 to five White Sox players threatened to expose the plot if the Sox won the American League pennant.

Charles Comiskey and Ban Johnson had always disliked one another, but the sudden remarks made by Johnson that gamblers were threatening to expose the White Sox players involved in a 1919 World Series plot widened the rift even further. Comiskey objected to Johnson's interview, raising the possibility that certain gamblers were trying to blackmail the White Sox into losing the 1920 pennant to Cleveland. Comiskey accused Johnson of attempting to sabotage the White Sox 1920 pennant run by breaking their morale at a critical point of the pennant race.

When Ban Johnson was informed of Comiskey's allegation that he was attempting to prevent the White Sox from winning the pennant, he responded that "Comiskey's charges are the vaporing of a vindictive man."

Johnson said, "Comiskey was quibbling over side issues and that all sides in baseball should help the grand jury get to the bottom of the scandal of fixed games."

"From public reports it would appear that an individual is grasping at straws in an effort to purify his position with the public," said Johnson. "A gentleman from the editorial staff of a Chicago daily newspaper called at my home last Wednesday night. He explained that he had little knowledge of baseball. In the course of conversation he said his office had a report that the White Sox dare not win the American League pennant, that certain players were in the grip of gamblers and should they win the fraud of last fall would be exposed. He wanted to know if I had learned of such reports. I replied there were vague rumors of that sort, but that they would not be given credence."

Johnson concluded his remarks by saying, "I am amazed that the papers should give ear and voice to the vaporizing of a man whose vindictiveness toward the president of the American League has been so long and so thoroughly known. This is not the time for quibbling and side issues. The integrity of professional baseball is on trial before the jury in Cook County and we are content to abide by its findings and decisions."[11]

As the clouds of doubt and scandal were quickly forming, everyone in baseball was beginning to take a public stand on the grand jury probe. National League president John Heydler said that the whole affair could have been avoided if White Sox manager Kid Gleason had taken prompt and proper action against the players under suspicion.

"Gleason could have done much to avoid all this," said Heydler. "From the information that I gathered in the East from a baseball writer, Gleason openly accused some of his players while the series was being played. Ray Schalk was called into the conference and he supported manager Gleason in his contention. If this is true Gleason should have taken the players under suspicion out of the game."[12]

The unnamed New York newspaper source that Heydler was referring to was undoubtedly Hugh Fullerton and the incident of confronting
his players was most probably his much ballyhooed verbal explosion in
the lobby of the Hotel Sinton in Cincinnati following game one.[13]

Meanwhile, Prosecutor Replogle was busy responding to the rumor
mill. He denied reports that White Sox players Buck Weaver and Fred
McMullin had been refused a hearing. "We barred no one," he said. "But
don't expect to call any Chicago players until the pennant race is settled."
Replogle also denied reports that every major league team had been implicated in gambling and throwing games in evidence already given to the
jury: "There are only one or two teams implicated thus far and just a few
players," he said.[14]

Charles Comiskey stated that if the White Sox win the American
League pennant then every member of the team would play in the World
Series. He said that he would give every player the benefit of doubt until
proven guilty. Therefore if any player was proven guilty, then he would
"be busted at once."[15]

Popular belief has been that Charles Comiskey's suspicions were far
out in front of his public position and that both Comiskey and Kid Gleason had been suspicious for some time of Eddie Cicotte as possibly being
involved in some sort of plot in the 1919 World Series. They had heard all
of the rumors, saw Rube Benton's grand jury testimony hit the newspapers, and now there was the incriminating story told by Bill Maharg in the
Philadelphia North American. Consequently, Comiskey decided it was time
to confront Cicotte personally.

Whether or not the following event actually happened is at most speculation. The event has always been vague in the actual details and a lot
that has been written about the event has simply evolved into acceptance
as fact. However, I mention the event because it has been so heavily dra-
matized and written about extensively over the years.

The popular theory advanced by many has it that Charles Comiskey
thought, as a result of contract negotiations and personal contact he had
with Cicotte, that he would be a weak link in a conspiracy cover-up. Therefore, sometime in the period between the last game that Cicotte pitched
on September 26 and the afternoon of September 28 when he was scheduled to testify in front of the grand jury, Comiskey arranged for Cicotte
to meet him in the loop office of his attorney, Al Austrian.

Furthermore, the popular theory holds that as soon as Cicotte arrived
at Austrian's office the psychological warfare was begun upon him. He was
asked to wait. After a half-hour passed, a secretary escorted him into a
conference room and again asked him to wait. After another half-hour

passed, the secretary returned and this time escorted him into an office where Comiskey, Austrian and Gleason waited for him. No one got up to greet Cicotte or shake his hand; they motioned him to sit in a chair and just stared at him. Soon after, Cicotte broke down and sobbed, then offered a confession.

Finally this unsubstantiated legend has it that Comiskey simply told him, "Tell it to the grand jury."[16]

Nonetheless, it is a fact that Comiskey somehow had coerced Cicotte and Joe Jackson to sign waivers of immunity and then had Al Austrian arrange for them to testify at the grand jury hearings. Austrian even escorted Joe Jackson to the hearing.

On September 28, 1920, Eddie Cicotte and Joe Jackson did tell it to the jury. Subsequently, their testimonies before the grand jury caused the roof to blow off in the allegations of an alleged scandal in the 1919 World Series.

Also testifying that day before the grand jury was a so-called mystery woman. Mrs. Henrietta Kelly, the mystery woman, owned apartment buildings, i.e., flats, in which some of the accused players lived. She is said to have heard Eddie Cicotte tell his brother after the first game, "I don't give a damn, I got mine."[17]

Before entering the grand jury room both Cicotte and Jackson made statements to Chief Justice Judge Charles McDonald. The statements to the grand jury were taken down by stenographers, but withheld from the press by State's Attorney Hoyne.

Also the exact nature of the information Charles Comiskey put before the grand jury was not disclosed either.

There was an air of suspense in the room as Eddie Cicotte took the stand. But after a few moments he broke down in tears and then told a heart-wrenching story of betrayal. One juror stated later, "He said again and again, he wished he wasn't mixed up in it."[18]

The following is a composite of Eddie Cicotte's testimony taken from several newspapers. Subsequently, in the various accounts printed of Cicotte's involvement in the alleged plot, all reported categorically that he accepted a $10,000 cash payment from gambling elements. However, a contradiction occurs about the degree of his on-field participation in the news reports of his testimony. In one printed version, Cicotte allegedly states that he threw softballs up to the plate. Yet in another version Cicotte states that he played to win at all costs.

Cicotte allegedly told the grand jury that he, Joe Jackson and six other teammates had conspired to throw games in the 1919 World Series.

The players implicated were pitcher Claude "Lefty" Williams, first baseman Arnold "Chick" Gandil, outfielder Oscar "Happy" Felsch, short-stop Charles "Swede" Risberg, infielder Fred McMullin and third base-man George "Buck" Weaver.

According to Cicotte's testimony, the bribes that each of those impli-cated were alleged to have accepted were Chick Gandil, $20,000; Fred McMullin, $15,000; Happy Felsch, $5,000; Lefty Williams, $10,000; Joe Jackson, $5,000; Buck Weaver, $5,000; Swede Risberg, $10,000; and him-self, $10,000.

The amount of money cleaned up by the alleged gambling syndicate on the World Series was close to $200,000. A man by the name of Hahn, located in Pittsburgh, was implicated as the brains of this operation. Abe Attell was implicated as his right-hand man. Bill Burns was used by the syndicate as the man who could reach Chick Gandil to sound out the var-ious players on the White Sox team. It was stated that Burns did business individually with every one of the eight White Sox players implicated. Cicotte, McMullin and Williams helped him in this respect.

The grand jurors questioned Cicotte as to how it was possible to throw a game.

"It is easy to throw a game," Cicotte said. "Just a slight hesitation on the part of the player will let a man get to base or make a run."

Sobbing, he then pleaded, "My God, think of my children." He went on:

> I played a crooked game and lost. I would do anything to undo it. I have lived a thousand years in the past year.
>
> Chick Gandil acted as the go-between in all the money deals.
>
> Risberg, Gandil and McMullin were at me for a week before the series started. They wanted me to go crooked. I needed the money. I had the wife and kids. They don't know this, and I don't know what they think.
>
> I had bought a farm. There was a $4,000 mortgage. I paid that off with crooked money.
>
> The eight of us — the eight under indictment — got together in my room three or four days before the series started. Gandil was master of the cere-monies. We talked about throwing the series, and decided we could get away with it. We agreed to do it.
>
> I was thinking of the wife and kids and how I needed the money. I told them to have the cash in advance. I did not want any checks. I didn't want any promises. I wanted the money in bills before I pitched a ball.
>
> We all talked quite a while about it. Yes all of us decided to do our best to throw the games to Cincinnati. Then Gandil and McMullin took us all one by one away from the others, and we talked turkey. They asked me my price. I told them $10,000, paid in advance.
>
> It was Gandil I was talking to. He wanted to give me some money at the time and the rest after the games were played and lost.

Cash in advance, not C.O.D., I reminded him. If you cannot trust me, I can't trust you. Pay or I play ball.

Well, the argument went on for some days. But I stood pat. I wanted $10,000, and I got it.

How I wish that I had not. The day before I went to Cincinnati I put it up squarely for the last time that there would be nothing doing unless I had the money.

That night I found the money under my pillow. I had sold out Chommy and the other boys to pay off a mortgage on a farm for the wife and kids.[19]

Then we arrive at the contradiction in Cicotte's testimony in regards to his level of on-field participation in the plot.

In the September 29, 1920, editions of both the *Cincinnati Enquirer* and the *Philadelphia Inquirer* the following testimony of Cicotte to the grand jury is printed as follows:

In the first game at Cincinnati I was knocked out of the box. I wasn't putting a thing on the ball. You could have read the trade mark on it when I lobbed it up to the plate.

In the fourth game played at Chicago which I also lost, I deliberately intercepted a throw from the outfield to the plate which might have cut off a run. I muffed the ball on purpose. At another time in the same game I purposely made a wild throw. All the runs scored against me were due to my own deliberate errors. I did not try to win.

Then in the September 30, 1920, edition of the *Philadelphia Inquirer* the following version of Cicotte's testimony in regard to his on-field involvement in the alleged plot was printed.

The first ball I pitched I wondered what the wife and kiddies would say if they ever found out I was a crook. I pitched the best ball I knew how after that first ball. But I lost because I was hit, not because I was throwing the game.

That afternoon Joe Jackson was led down to the grand jury room through a gauntlet of reporters and cameramen. He shed no tears, but hung his head and covered his face. Prosecutor Replogle nursed him along through the crowd. He then entered the grand jury room and corroborated the testimony of Cicotte in every detail.

Jackson stated to the jury that Lefty Williams drew him into the plot.

"When Claude Williams unfolded the plan to give the series to the Cincinnati Reds, I demanded $20,000 for my share. We had several conferences and squabbles over the amount, but I finally consented to take the $5,000. Williams told me that we were all getting the same. Had I known that some of the others were getting $10,000 I would have held out for $20,000."[20]

Jackson's story was really one of being double-crossed.

His price was $20,000. He told the jury that all he had to do was when hits meant runs, he either struck out or just tapped the ball for an easy out.

He found $5,000 on his bed before the series started. Unlike Cicotte who mistrusted the go-betweens, he accepted their word that the $15,000 would "be made up after they had cashed in." After they cashed in he was told, "Start to squeal and see where you get off."

Jackson described his confession to the grand jury.

> I heard I had been indicted. I decided these men could not put anything over on me. I called up Judge McDonald [Chief Justice Charles A. McDonald of the Criminal Court] and told him I was an honest man. He said, "I know you are not," and hung up the receiver.
>
> I figured that somebody had squawked and that the place for me was the ground floor. I went over to tell what I knew.
>
> I got in there and said, I got $5,000 and they promised me $20,000. Lefty Williams handed it to me in a dirty envelope.

The grand jury was recessed for the day.

Jackson was before the grand jury for nearly two hours. When he came out he was walking erect and smiling.

Following their testimony Cicotte and Jackson were taken into custody and charged with conspiracy to commit an illegal act. Indictments were returned against them and the other five active White Sox players and one former player Chick Gandil.

Joe Jackson left the Criminal Court Building in the charge of bailiffs. He had asked for protection from the court, as he was fearful that Swede Risberg would cause him physical harm for testifying. The bailiffs refused to let the press talk with him. They stated that they were taking him home and then quickly drove off in a taxi. There is no record of any newsboy confronting Joe Jackson with the legendary words, "Say it ain't so, Joe."

Assistant State Attorney Hartley Replogle announced penalties that the indicted seven active ball players and one retired ball player could face provided for under new state law were from one to five years in the penitentiary and a fine of not more than $10,000.

The confessions of Cicotte and Jackson put the testimony of other witnesses that had appeared before the jury earlier in the background. However, the state attorney's office announced that soon an investigation would begin that would involve Bill Maharg, former boxer Bill Burns, a retired ball player now promoting the oil industry of Texas, and Abe Attell who was indicated by Cicotte and Jackson as the engineer of the double-cross.

Immediately following the testimony of Cicotte and Jackson, Charles A. Comiskey, the "Old Roman" of baseball, suspended every player named, thereby throwing out of the window his American League pennant chances in 1920.

Comiskey, seated amidst his crumbling empire at Comiskey Park as the grand jury was voting their true bills charging a conspiracy had taken place, notified the players of their suspensions via the following telegram.

> You and each of you are hereby notified of your indefinite suspension as a member of the Chicago American League Baseball Club.
>
> Your suspension is brought about by information which has just come to me directly involving you and each of you in the baseball scandal (now being investigated by the grand jury of Cook county) resulting from the World's Series of 1919.
>
> If you are innocent of any wrong doing, you and each of you will be reinstated: if you are guilty you will be retired from organized baseball for the rest of your lives if I can accomplish it.
>
> Until there is a finality to this investigation it is due to the public that I take this action, even though it costs Chicago the pennant.[21]

Comiskey in tears, his team in ruins that he had labored so hard to build, paid off Cicotte and Jackson on the spot and announced that checks for pay due the other suspended players would be sent immediately.

Comiskey told the press that the players that he had scrapped would have been worth $230,000 on the trade market. According to his own valuations he could have fetched $50,000 a piece for Jackson, Weaver and Felsch.

As the news of Comiskey's predicament hit the wires, contemporaries attempted to come to his aid, even if only symbolically.

Harry Frazee, president of the Boston Red Sox, said that he believed that it was duty of each club in the American League to give one of its players to the Chicago White Sox to assist in its rehabilitation, should the indicted Chicago players be found guilty.

The owners of the New York Yankees, Jacob Ruppert and T. L. Huston, wired Comiskey and offered to give players with whom he could finish the season, including Babe Ruth!

When informed of the Yankees' offer Comiskey replied, "It's a splendid offer and one I appreciate from the bottom of my heart, but I'm afraid there is no way I can accept it."[22]

In reality the American League rules in effect in 1920 would not have allowed it. The rules stated that no trades or transfers of players could be made after August 31.

With his voice trembling, Comiskey said, "This was the first time scandal had touched his family and that it distressed him too much to talk about it."

New York Giants manager John J. McGraw had been in Chicago that day awaiting the call to testify the next day. Following the recess of the court, he stood in the hallway of the Criminal Courts Building with veteran Chicago newsman John O'Leary and editorialized to all that would listen.

"That it was enough to break an old ball player's heart — this damn crookedness among men who make more in a week than we made in a year when we fought with our bare hands to keep the game clean."

"Wrong," roared McGraw. "Wrong. It's a damn outrage. I've had a hunch on this a long time and take it from me John, before I get through I'll make baseball an unpopular place for crooks."[23]

Notwithstanding the shocking events that occurred at the grand jury hearing on September 28, the American League pennant race continued.

The Cleveland Indians that day defeated the St. Louis Browns 9-5 as Jim Bagby won his 30th game of the season. In the losing effort for the Browns George Sisler had two hits, thereby setting a new American League record of 250 hits in a single season.

The Indians now had a one-game lead over the decimated White Sox in the American League race and would not look back.

Also in Chicago that day the National Commission reversed its decision of the previous day and at the request of Cleveland Indians President Jim Dunn, moved the opening games of the 1920 World Series to begin in Brooklyn on October 5 to give the additional time to Dunn that he required constructing temporary seats. Therefore the games to be played in the American League park, either Cleveland or Chicago, would begin on October 8.

Finally, Jim Dunn telegraphed the Brooklyn club asking that Joe Sewell be permitted to play at shortstop for the Indians in the World Series in the event they win the American League pennant. Sewell had only recently joined the team and his contract had not been promulgated prior to the August 31 deadline.

Sewell had succeeded the Indians' regular shortstop Ray Chapman, who while at bat was hit in the left temple with a pitch thrown by Yankees pitcher Carl Mays in a game played on August 16, then had tragically died the next day as a result of a fractured skull.

On the morning of September 29 newspapers all over the land carried a collage of the eight present and former White Sox players who had been indicted. Some papers like the *Chicago American* and *Cincinnati Enquirer* put the faces of the accused players on the front page. Others, such as the *Philadelphia Inquirer*, located the players' pictures, which were tantamount to mug shots, to the sports pages. But all the papers carried the details of the previous day's grand jury hearings and stories of the confessions of Eddie Cicotte and Joe Jackson for all to see. While most of the testimony of Cicotte and Jackson was kept in secrecy, unofficial accounts were filtering through to the press.

Prior to testifying before the grand jury, Claude "Lefty" Williams made a sworn statement to Charles Comiskey's attorney, Al Austrian. Williams was then hustled into the grand jury room to tell his story to the jurors. That grand jury testimony was subsequently lost and could not be entered into evidence when the eight accused players were brought to trial.

Williams's statement to Austrian read in part:

> This situation was first brought up to me in New York. Gandil called me to one side, out in front of the Hotel Ansonia, and asked me if anybody had approached me about the World's Series; and I said, "Just what do you mean?" He says, "The Series may be fixed; if it is fixed what would you do about it? Would you take an active part or what?" I says, "I'm in no position to say right now." I says, "I will give you my answer later after thinking it over."
>
> After coming back to Chicago I was called to the Warner Hotel, where the eight members that are named — not eight, I will take that back; I will name them for you — Eddie Cicotte, Chick Gandil, Buck Weaver and Happy Felsch and two fellows introduced as Brown and Sullivan —

> AUSTRIAN: They were the gamblers.
> WILLIAMS: They were supposed to be the gamblers.
> AUSTRIAN: What names were used?
> WILLIAMS: Brown and Sullivan, supposed to be the gamblers or fellows that were fixing it for the gamblers, one of the two, they didn't say which. They said they were from Boston. They wanted us to throw the series to Cincinnati for $5,000.
> AUSTRIAN: Apiece?
> WILLIAMS: Yes. And I said that wasn't enough money to fool with and I was informed that whether or not I took any action the games would be fixed.
> AUSTRIAN: Who informed you of that?
> WILLIAMS: Chick Gandil.
> AUSTRIAN: Right then and there?

WILLIAMS: No, not right then and there; right after that, just as I
    got in the hall. So I told him anything they did would be agree-
    able with me; if it was going to be done anyway, that I had no
    money and I might as well get what I could.
WILLIAMS: I haven't seen those gamblers from that day to this.
    Gandil told me that we were supposed to get —
AUSTRIAN: What was it?
WILLIAMS: I was supposed to get $10,000 after the second game when
    we got back to Chicago, and I didn't get this until after the fourth
    game, and he then said that the gamblers had called it off; and
    I figured then that there was a double-cross some place. On the
    second trip to Cincinnati, Cicotte and I had a conference. I told
    him that we were double-crossed and that I was going to win if
    there was any possible chance. Cicotte said he was the same way.
    Gandil informed me in Cincinnati that Bill Burns and Abe Attell
    were fixing it so that we could get $100,000 making $20,000
    more. That I never received.[24]

Williams concluded his session before the White Sox attorney by stating that when the team returned to Cincinnati a meeting of several players was held at the hotel in Chick Gandil's room. Those in attendance
included Gandil, Buck Weaver, Happy Felsch and himself.

Gandil stated that he was going after Burns and Attell in regards to
the money that was due the players. However, once again Williams
repeated that the only payment he ever received was the $10,000 after the
fourth game of which he gave $5,000 to Jackson.

Following Williams' testimony, the rumor mill was working over-
time. It was believed that Williams had told the jurors that Chick Gandil
had buried a box, which may have contained the balance of the $100,000
due to the players.

Also testifying before the jury that day was Giants manager John
McGraw and John A. Heydler, president of the National League.

Heydler was direct in his denial that information had ever reached
him that attempts had been made to fix the approaching 1920 World Series.

Heydler did not testify in regard to the alleged fix in the Chicago-
Philadelphia game of August 31, the incident that led to the 1919 World
Series inquiry by the jury.

He did, however, relate a rather amusing story to the jury in which
a player attempting to throw a game really helped to win it. Heydler stated
that Lee Magee had confessed to him and William Veeck, president of the
Chicago Cubs, that he took part in throwing several games.

"In July, 1918, Magee was playing second base for Cincinnati against
Boston. He came to bat with two out, hit an easy grounder, which took a

bad bounce and he was safe. He was ordered to steal second and ambled down. When half way to second, he stopped, but Art Wilson made a wild throw and Magee had to go on to third. He might have scored with the tying run, I think if he had tried, but he didn't. Then Edd Roush knocked a home run. Magee had to come in with the tying run and Roush's run of course, won the game."[25]

When Heydler left the jury room the jurors applauded him.

"We want to thank you for giving your time to help in this investigation," said jury foreman Harry Brigham.

Heydler replied, "We're the ones who should be thanking you. When a jury does what you have done for baseball, it's time for baseball to thank you."

In an impromptu press conference, jury foreman Brigham summed up the opinion of the grand jury in regard to the alleged 1919 World Series scandal.

> The eight players indicted are apparently only tools of a gambling ring. The ramifications of this extend everywhere that professional baseball is known.
>
> It is plainly evident that some of these boys yielded to the influence of those whose names doubtless will appear in the list of defendants later on.
>
> I sympathize with some of them. They were foolish, unsophisticated country boys who yielded to the temptations placed in their path by professional gamblers.
>
> I hope that the cleansing process of this investigation will extend to all the sore spots in the sporting world.[26]

Brigham finished with a statement that although the grand jury's normal period of office would expire the next day, the jurors' term would be continued indefinitely until the baseball investigation was complete.

Assistant State Attorney Hartley Replogle stated, "The details of charges against the eight White Sox players have not been completed." He added that indictments would probably be drawn that day, and that they might contain several counts.[27]

Also Replogle remarked that under Illinois statutes the time limit for bettors to bring suits in order to recover losses on last year's World Series expired six months ago. There was, however, another provision for a third party to bring a suit to recover twice the amount lost, half of which would go to the county and half to the informer.

With the grand jury investigation winding down, around the baseball world various dignitaries were being sought out for statements.

When Cincinnati Reds manager Pat Moran was sought out by the press for a statement in regard to the news out of Chicago, he simply stated,

"The bribe money was wasted. The Reds would have beat the White Sox regardless."[28]

Charles H. Ebbets, owner of the National League pennant-clinching Brooklyn Robins, remarked to the press, "I would be against playing the Sox even if it meant there would be no World Series this fall."[29]

Ban Johnson, president of the American League, said, "It takes the breath away from me. I'll have to have more time to think it over, and will make a formal statement later."[30]

Charles Comiskey, over the initial shock of the previous day, was picking up the pieces and making plans as the White Sox prepared to play the final three games of the season in St. Louis.

"We are far from through. We have the nucleus of another championship team with the remainder of the old world's championship team."[31]

He named veterans Eddie Collins and John Collins, Ray Schalk, Urban (Red) Faber, Dick Kerr, Eddie Murphy, Nemo Leibold and Amos Strunk, and declared that with the addition of players such as Clarence Hodge, Bob Falk, Harvey McClellan and Ted Jourdan, "I guess we can go along and win the championship yet."

But at the same time, Harry Grabner, secretary of the White Sox, was not so optimistic. He announced to the press that "the club would play out the schedule to the end if it had to employ Chinamen to fill the vacancies on the team."[32]

To win the pennant the White Sox would need to beat the Browns in all three remaining games and the Indians would need to lose two of their final four games on the remainder of the schedule.

But the Sox's chances were rapidly slipping away as the Indians once again pounded the Browns 10-2, thereby sweeping the four-game series and opening up a 1½-game lead with four games left to play.

Also, there was renewed talk of scandal on the club. Some of the White Sox players not indicted were suddenly calling for a probe of the 1920 season. There was growing concern that some of the players accused of dumping last year's World Series were also attempting to prevent the Sox from winning the pennant this year.

One player who wanted to go unnamed (probably Eddie Collins) told the press,

> When we started on our last Eastern trip we had every reason to believe we would win the pennant. Suddenly Williams and Cicotte seemed to go bad without any reason. Some of us talked it over and agreed it looked like they were grooving the ball.
>
> Then Jackson, Felsch and Risberg began dumping the ball to the infield every time they came to bat when we had a chance to get runs.

We thought at first they might just be in a slump, but when some of us compared notes regarding the pitching and hitting we became more than suspicious.

It may as well be stated that some of us believe that ever since the last World's Series that we were sold by Cicotte and others.

Well when the same men we suspected crossing us at that time began to go bad on the last Eastern trip we decided there must have been another sell-out. Had we played anything like our regular game we would have come home with the pennant clinched.[33]

Sox pitcher Urban "Red" Faber said, "The playing of the Sox on the Eastern trip made some of the other believe that something was crooked."

"It looks like we were double-crossed in the World's Series last year and in the pennant race this year, but we are not through yet."[34]

As talk of scandal and grand jury hearings swept across the country on September 29, at Shibe Park in Philadelphia before 15,000 fans, the New York Yankees closed out their season by sweeping a double header from the Athletics 7-3 and 9-4. In the ninth inning of the first game Babe Ruth hit his 54th home run of the season.

That evening Buck Weaver called up Assistant State Attorney Replogle and discussed possible arrangements to go before the grand jury and confess his connection with the scandal in the series. Weaver assured Replogle he would get in touch with him the following day and in the meantime would try to persuade Fred McMullin, also under indictment, to accompany him.

That weekend in their final three-game series with St. Louis the Chicago White Sox won just one game, thereby finishing the season in second place two games behind Cleveland.

On September 30 the Cleveland Indians went to Detroit, began their final series of the season and won two out of four games to clinch the pennant.

Unlike the unfair doubt cast on the 1919 World Series victory of the Cincinnati Reds, surprisingly there has never been any suggestion that the Cleveland Indians 1920 American League pennant was given to them through scandal and game fixing by the Chicago White Sox. A double standard? You bet.

Final American League Standings 1920

Team	Won	Lost	GB	PCT.
Cleveland	98	56		.636
Chicago	96	58	2	.623

Team	Won	Lost	GB	PCT.
New York	95	59	3	.617
St. Louis	76	77	21½	.497
Boston	72	81	25½	.471
Washington	68	84	29	.447
Detroit	61	93	37	.396
Philadelphia	48	106	50	.312

With the 1920 World Series about to begin, rumors began to circulate that the same gambling elements that had tampered with the 1919 World Series were attempting to do it again.

Reports were made to newspapers including the *New York Evening Sun*, that several members of the Brooklyn Robins were approached about fixing games. In New York, Robins' Captain Zack Wheat indignantly denied that any of the Brooklyn players had been approached. None-the-less Kings County District Attorney Harry B. Lewis quickly summoned several Brooklyn players and immediately started an investigation.

CHAPTER TWELVE

Setting the Record Straight

In November 1920 the voters of Illinois cast election ballots that resulted in a change in the district attorney's office in Cook County. Consequently, State Attorneys Hoyne, Replogle and others who had presented the conspiracy evidence to the grand jury in September were now out of office. Subsequently, the trial would be delayed.

However, later in November 1920 indictments were brought against seven former White Sox players, Eddie Cicotte, Happy Felsch, Chick Gandil, Joe Jackson, Swede Risberg, Bucky Weaver and Lefty Williams, in charges of participating in a conspiracy to throw the 1919 World Series. Charges against Fred McMullin were dropped for lack of evidence.

Not one of the known gamblers— Abe Attell, Billy Burns, Bill Maharg or the elusive Mr. Hahn from either Cincinnati or Pittsburgh, not Mr. Brown, or even Joseph Sullivan from Boston — alleged to be in on, or that had formulated the plot, were indicted.

Also there was no indictment returned on Arnold Rothstein who was, depending on various popular versions of his involvement, alleged to be the mastermind of the plot, or the financier of the plot or both. Even though F. Scott Fitzgerald later romanticized the alleged involvement of Arnold Rothstein in *The Great Gatsby*, Rothstein was never legally proven guilty of any crime and was never charged with any crime involving the 1919 World Series.

At about the same time that the indictments against the players were

being returned, the National Commission was disbanded by the club owners in favor of an independent commissioner's office. Therefore on November 12, 1920, Judge Kenesaw Mountain Landis was appointed as the first
Commissioner of Baseball.

Landis, who was 53 years old when appointed commissioner, was a
federal judge who had gained fame in the 1907 federal anti-trust case
against Standard Oil.

In June 1921 a conspiracy trial would begin in the Chicago courtroom
of Judge Dever for the seven former White Sox players alleged to have par-
ticipated in a conspiracy to throw the 1919 World Series. However, on
August 2, 1921, all seven players were acquitted of any wrongdoing (Eddie
Cicotte, Happy Felsch, Chick Gandil, Joe Jackson, Swede Risberg, Buck
Weaver and Lefty Williams).

The not-guilty verdict was reinforced by the fact that the confession
statements of the players had disappeared from the district attorney's files.

Immediately following the trial there were rumors that Arnold Rothstein had paid off the outgoing Illinois district attorneys in the sum of
$10,000 to steal the incriminating documents against the White Sox play-
ers. Then four years later the documents somehow were discovered in the
files of none other than White Sox owner Charles A. Comiskey.

On August 4, 1921, two days after the not-guilty verdicts were
returned in the conspiracy trial, the moody Judge Landis (an avid White
Sox fan) issued a lifetime ban from baseball on all eight former players,
including nonindicted player Fred McMullin, thereby ending their careers
in baseball permanently. Landis' edict that lives in infamy is here repro-
duced.

"Regardless of the verdict of juries, no player that throws a ball game,
no player that entertains proposals or promises to throw a game, no player
that sits in a conference with a bunch of crooked players and gamblers
where the ways and means of throwing games are discussed, and does not
promptly tell his club about it, will ever play professional baseball."

So it was all over. Eight players had their careers in major league baseball brought to an end permanently and the debate of what actually took
place in the 1919 World Series began and continues until this very day.

That debate can be highly personal. I for one grew up in Cincinnati
and as a child had bitter feelings about the never ending challenge to the
validity of the Reds' victory in the 1919 World Series. As a matter of fact,
I still do.

Each baseball season in the early 1950s I looked forward to my initial outing to Crosley Field (formerly Redland Field) to see the Reds play.
I also looked forward with great expectations to having the opportunity

to purchase my copy of the Cincinnati Reds yearbook at the ball park's souvenir stands.

Paging through my new Reds yearbook for the first time was always an exciting event. For some reason I just loved the smell and feel of the slick pages. I could hardly wait to arrive at the pages containing the pictures and statistics of my favorite players, "Big Klu" (Ted Kluszewski), Roy McMillan, Wally Post, Hershell Freeman, etc. I knew that Kluszewski had hit 40 home runs in the 1953 season, but I did not consider it official until I saw it there in black and white in the 1954 yearbook.

Still, in the journey through the yearbook pages it would be necessary each year to be reminded that something had happened in the history of the Cincinnati Reds that was very unpleasant. Something that got your attention and made you angry.

About midway through the 1954, 1955, and 1956 editions of the Reds yearbook, the publishers had included one page dedicated to each of the three World Series that the Reds had played in up to that point in time. While both the layouts for the 1939 and 1940 World Series appeared exciting and aquatinted you with Reds heroes from another era such as Bucky Walters, Ernie Lombardi and Frank McCormick, the page continuing the reference to the 1919 World Series appeared most intimidating. It got your attention.

The banner headlines on the page screamed out words to the effect of "REDS DEFEAT BLACKSOX!" Included in the spread were old newspaper headlines declaring a scandal and a couple of box scores superimposed on each other. The whole layout looked grossly out of place. Furthermore it generated more questions about the event than it provided information.

For some reason I just always wanted to rip that damn page out of the yearbook and throw it away. The whole thing just made you a little ill.

I would buy yearbooks of visiting teams too. The Brooklyn Dodgers yearbook didn't contain any such blemishes on their history. I didn't see any in the Chicago Cubs yearbook or Milwaukee Braves yearbook either.

To this day, I cannot understand why Reds owner Powell Crosley, Jr., and General manager Gabe Paul, such astute baseball executives, would have allowed such organizational self-flagellation to be printed in the ball club's most important marketing tool. The way the 1919 World Series was presented in the Reds yearbooks during the early 1950s was totally self-defeating and reinforced a lot of misinformation about the series that fans had been unjustly conditioned to accept as facts. But most unfortunate of all about the way the 1919 World Series was presented in those yearbooks is that it resulted in a blatant show of organizational disrespect, if not outright contempt, for the players on the 1919 World Champion Cincinnati Reds team.

When you reduce the reason for the mischief in the 1919 World Series to its most common denominator you arrive at the conclusion that Charles A. Comiskey was responsible for his own downfall. Consider the temptation of superstar Joe Jackson being paid a meager $6,000 a year by Comiskey to accept a bribe of $5,000, when his contemporaries in the American League such as Ty Cobb and Tris Speaker were making three times that amount in their contracts. Make no mistake about it, if there really is a taint on the series it cannot with good conscience be assigned solely to the alleged actions of Eddie Cicotte, Lefty Williams, Chick Gandil and the others, but rather to the archaic labor relations of the "Noble Roman" of baseball. However, it is grossly unfair to allow the tarnish to remain on the stunning hard-fought victory of the Cincinnati Reds in the 1919 World Series that resulted from miserly ways of Charles Comiskey.

A World Series is a lot harder to fix than one would initially think or that was offered as testimony in the 1920 grand jury hearings.

For example in a Super Bowl a player can drop a pass in the end zone, fumble a kick off, let his defensive counterpart run rampant over him all day. There are scores of unsuspicious ways to let down on the field.

But in a World Series there is a visibility factor. You have let down the level of your play for anywhere from four to seven days in a row and that is a pretty tall order for any player with ulterior motives about not playing to the best of their ability.

The 1919 Cincinnati Reds were more than capable of winning the World Series over the Chicago White Sox regardless if a conspiracy existed. The 1919 Cincinnati Reds' winning percentage of .686 (96-44) is the highest in the club's history. It was even a higher winning percentage than the 1975 edition of the Big Red Machine that steamrolled to the National League Western Division Crown with a winning percentage of .667 (108-54) while outdistancing the second place Los Angeles Dodgers by 20 games.

Now it would be ludicrous to deny the considerable body of circumstantial evidence that suggests several of the White Sox players accepted bribes in the 1919 World Series. The September 1920 grand jury testimony of Eddie Cicotte, Joe Jackson and Lefty Williams is rather conclusive and was corroborated by Bill Maharg in the press.

However, to what end the bribes of the White Sox players implicated in the alleged conspiracy actually resulted in sub-par play leading to White Sox defeats in various games in the World Series is highly subjective.

Furthermore, right from the start in the conspiracy theory there is a substantial conflict in how arrangements for the alleged fix were made. In the grand jury testimony of New York Giant pitcher Rube Benton is stated,

"Certain players on the White Sox team had visited Pittsburgh before the series was played and made arrangements to throw games for a price."

However, in almost every version of the alleged event told over the past 81 years, from Ward and Burns in their PBS series *Baseball* to the Hollywood version of *Eight Men Out*, the setting for the agreement on the conspiracy is the Ansonia Hotel in New York City a few weeks before the series.

The fact is that no one really knows for sure where and when the discussion for an alleged conspiracy took place or even if it took place at all in the ways commonly accepted.

Then the entire conspiracy theory in a nutshell, formed in retrospect, is the sportswriters considered the White Sox a more formidable team than the Reds, so when huge amounts of money were suddenly being bet on the Reds to win the series, something smelled.

After the fact, starting in September 1920 and continuing through this very day, sportswriters and those convinced of the conspiracy have built a retrospective analysis based on an inventory of what they allege were various suspicious on-field actions of several White Sox players, thereby supporting their theory that something was terribly wrong in the 1919 World Series.

This after-the-fact inventory of indictment against the players includes shoddy pitching by Eddie Cicotte in game one. In the third game Chick Gandil hesitated on the base paths running from second to third. In the fourth game Eddie Cicotte made two critical errors, one cutting off a throw from Joe Jackson in the outfield, that gave the Reds openings. Happy Felsch made a throwing error in game five. Lefty Williams did not pitch up to his ability in the three games he started. In game two Williams walked six batters; in game five he gave up four runs to the Reds in the sixth inning. Then after being chased from the mound in the first inning of the eighth game after giving up two singles and two doubles, Williams finished the series with a 6.61 ERA. Lastly Joe Jackson is accused of slowing down on balls that he should have stopped throughout the series and of not hitting when it counted.

The accepted premise that the list of on-field actions mentioned above establishes definitive truth of a conspiracy to throw the series is a fallacy. The results from the actions and plays mentioned in the conspiracy theory are simply inconclusive and incapable of establishing truth in consequences adverse to the ultimate outcome of a World Series played out over the course of eight games.

This weak inventory of less then ten plays considered suspicious is a classic case of the tail wagging the dog. The Cincinnati Reds outplayed the

White Sox in every statistical category in the 1919 World Series. Yet for over 80 years now, the Reds have been subjected to a doubt cast on their brilliant victory by several post–World War I sportswriters who were in a position to lose their credibility as a result of picking the White Sox to win the series unless they proved relevance of those ten suspicious plays.

Such was the case with Hugh Fullerton who was unrelenting in getting his conclusion accepted of a conspiracy in the 1919 World Series. In his columns he played to the gallery of public opinion using sentiment rather than fact to arouse emotions of the multitudes to get them to accept that a conspiracy occurred in the series without presenting good evidence of such.

In actuality there is so little evidence to cry foul in a World Series that included eight games, 71.5 innings, 514 at bats, 123 hits, 137 runners advanced, 55 runs, 40 earned runs, 19 errors, 12 stolen bases, 52 strikeouts, 40 bases on balls, 3 shutouts and 10 complete games.

Furthermore, when one examines separately the level of involvement for each one of the eight White Sox players that were indicted by the grand jury away from the collective core of the less than ten suspicious plays, their individual involvement appears to be more passive than blatantly corrupt.

In fact as the conspiracy trial began in 1921, Buck Weaver, claiming that he was no more than an accessory to a conspiracy, requested that he be tried separately from the other six White Sox defendants. Had the court granted this motion, it is highly possible that Joe Jackson may have also requested a separate trial.

Now the core of the conspiracy would be reduced to just five players and, outside of the case that can possibly be made against the two pitchers Cicotte and Williams, the entire alleged conspiracy breaks down and becomes almost too narrow to gauge any direct influence from on-field actions of players in the outcomes of the games.

New York Giants manager John McGraw was so convinced of Buck Weaver's innocence that he was waiting for the trial to end in 1921 so that he could sign Weaver to play third base for him.

No one would argue that there is not substantial evidence to suggest that Chick Gandil was rotten to the core. In fact, the record suggests the Gandil was influenced by gambling elements throughout his entire major league career. Furthermore, the evidence is rather convincing that Gandil may have been the one who arranged the whole affair in the 1919 World Series with gambler Bill Burns. But the evidence to state for certain that Gandil was actively seeking ways each day on the field to throw games and the series is skeptical.

Right from the start the evidence of an off-field conspiracy by some of the players is much more convincing than the evidence of an on-field conspiracy. Such is the case with Chick Gandil.

Gandil did not quit baseball after the 1919 season as is often stated by the conspiracy theory devotees to this very day, including Ward and Burns. Furthermore, Gandil's alleged total take in bribes from gamblers in the World Series is even in dispute to whether it was $20,000 or $35,000.

Chick Gandil did not report for spring training in March 1920 because of a contract dispute with White Sox owner Charles Comiskey, not because he was living "the life of Riley" on his funny money from throwing games.

Chick Gandil's involvement in the alleged conspiracy in the 1919 World Series, however, remains puzzling when considering his level of play. The most popular episode advanced as evidence of Gandil attempting to throw a game was his hesitation running from second to third in the second inning of game three. What makes this one incident so shallow is the fact that Gandil had just got the hit that scored Happy Felsch, giving the Sox the lead in the game. Subsequently, Gandil could have remained at first, but as Greasy Neale was attempting to throw Felsch out at the plate, Gandil broke out in a mad dash for second. Then, of course, the controversial play occurred next with Gandil being thrown out at third on a late throw from Ray Fisher to Heinie Groh. However, outside of this one incident there is no other on-field play by Gandil that is suspect in the entire eight games in the series.

While Gandil, a lifetime .277 hitter, hit just .233 in the series, his five RBIs were second on the team to Joe Jackson's six. Defensively he made one error and his fielding average .988 was second highest of all the White Sox players who played in all eight games. In fact his 1919 series fielding average was higher than that during his appearance in the 1917 World Series (.986). Also the fact remains and is often overlooked that it was Gandil who delivered game deciding hits in the White Sox victories in game three and game six of the 1919 World Series.

Whatever Gandil's level of off-field involvement in a conspiracy to throw the series may have been, it still begs the question of what his motivation would be for delaying the defeat of the White Sox?

Lefty Williams stated to the grand jury that on the train ride back to Cincinnati following game five he told Eddie Cicotte that he was going to win if there was any way possible. He stated that Cicotte, sensing a double-cross by gamblers, felt the same way. Regardless if Williams was in or out of a conspiracy at this point it didn't mean very much, the Reds were leading the series 4-1 and the White Sox were on the verge of elimination.

Lefty Williams's performance in the series with an 0-3 won-lost record and 6.61 ERA is without a doubt a hapless one and is indefensible. As a result of Williams's horrible pitching performance he usually gets the rap of being the most suspect of the two pitchers implicated in the alleged series scandal. However, the fact remains that in the 1917 World Series in which the White Sox beat the New York Giants 4-2, Lefty Williams pitched only one inning which resulted in an ERA of 9.00. Williams was a young pitcher, 26 years old, and simply stated, may have not been a money pitcher either.

But because Lefty Williams had a poor performance on the mound in the 1919 World Series there is no mercy in the judgment heaped upon him. The pitching performance of Claude "Lefty" Williams in the 1919 World Series may have been a bad one, but his overall performance does not qualify as unusual in the fall classic when one takes a look at the record book.

In 1916 future Hall of Fame member Rube Marquard pitching for the Brooklyn Robins had a won-lost record of 0-2 and an ERA of 4.91 as the Robins lost the series to the Boston Red Sox 4-1. In 1954 Bob Lemon, another Hall of Fame member, had a terrific season for the Cleveland Indians, posting a record of 23-7. However, in the 1954 World Series as the New York Giants swept the Indians 4-0, Lemon was hit hard. He finished the series with a 0-2 record and an ERA of 6.75, having given up 16 hits in 13⅓ innings while walking eight batters.

The most notorious case of a pitcher who had good regular seasons but could not buy a win in the World Series is the Brooklyn Dodgers' Don Newcombe. Big Newk pitched in three World Series following remarkable regular seasons on the hill. Despite strong won-lost records in 1949 (17-8), 1955 (20-5) and 1956 (27-7), Newcombe had a combined World Series won-lost record of 0-4 and a bulging ERA of 8.59!

Lefty Williams ran into trouble in the fourth inning of the second game as a result of walking three Reds batters. Of course the conspiracy theory has it that because Williams was having control problems he was actually throwing the game. Yet when Dutch Ruether ran into trouble in the top of the fifth inning during game six by walking the first two White Sox batters, no mention of something irregular in his control was speculated then or now.

The double standard for play in the series is constant in the conspiracy theory argument. If a White Sox player bobbles a grounder then the fix is in; if a Reds player drops a fly then he simply misjudged the ball.

One of the more interesting aspects of the legend of Williams in the series is the report of alleged death threats supposedly made on his life or that of his wife prior to game eight by agents of Arnold Rothstein. This legend was portrayed rather dramatically in the film *Eight Men Out*. However, the death incidents have never been corroborated. Furthermore, as the grand jury did not for some unknown reason summon Rothstein, the alleged financier of the conspiracy, to testify, this entire affair is nothing more than speculation. It was without a doubt one of the most crucial elements of evidence necessary to prove a conspiracy in the 1919 World Series. But it does not exist.

By the most far-reaching definitions, the on-field actions of Lefty Williams alone do not establish his participation in a conspiracy. By definition a conspiracy is a combining or acting together to perform an illegal, treacherous or evil act. All of Williams' actions implied in the conspiracy theory do not positively and unequivocally show that he attempted to throw any game in the series. Pitchers have bad games and sometimes pitch several bad games in a row. It had happened in previous World Series and happened in later World Series too.

Whether Lefty Williams was beaten because he let down or because the Reds simply were on a tear and hit him hard are both subjective. I merely suggest that Williams' poor performance was really a matter of a little of both these circumstances occurring simultaneously.

Eddie Cicotte's 1917 World Series performance in which he had a won-lost record of 1-1 and an ERA of 1.96 for 23 innings was not that much different than that of his 1919 World Series performance (1-2) with an ERA of 2.91 for 21.2 innings. In fact a case could be made that Cicotte pitched pretty well in the series.

Eddie Cicotte is a case of mixed speculation as to his actual degree of his alleged off-field involvement and his on-field participation in a fix. It should be considered that after Cicotte was bombarded by the hard hitting of the Reds in game one, he pitched game four in which he lost to Jimmy Ring 2-0 with two days rest and then pitched game seven in which he won against Slim Sallee 4-1 with three days rest.

One glaring fact that is totally overlooked or just ignored by conspiracy theory devotees is that in game seven with the White Sox facing elimination being down in the series 4-2, Cicotte pitched a masterful game and the Reds left nine men on base. It is very apparent that with Cicotte giving it all he had and the rest of the Sox playing flawless ball, they were determined to win that game and return the series to Chicago. If a conspiracy existed at that point then it made no sense at all to continue any further play.

The conspiracy theorists constantly point out that Cicotte was considered a master of control. So how can anyone suggest that his control was suspect in the 1919 World Series where he only walked a total of five batters in 21.2 innings? Jimmy Ring of the Reds walked six batters in only 14 innings and Dutch Ruether walked four in 14 innings.

As for the case against Cicotte of being responsible for the White Sox losing games in the series, it all simply does not add up. In the final analysis Cicotte's ERA in the series was just 2.91 for 21.2 innings pitched, which would be considered outstanding when compared to the statistics of any World Series pitcher on record, then or now.

Denny McLain, a 30-game winner (31-6) for the 1968 Detroit Tigers, had a 1-2 record in the 1968 World Series with an 3.24 ERA for just 16.2 innings pitched. In the 1980 World Series, Steve Charlton, pitching for the Philadelphia Phillies, was 2-0 with an ERA of 2.40 for only 15 innings pitched.

There is serious doubt on what the real story was that Cicotte told the grand jury. Was it as reported on September 29 that in the first game he put nothing on the ball, that it was possible to count the seams? Or was it as reported on September 30, that "I pitched the best ball I knew how after that first ball. But I lost because I was hit, not because I was throwing the game."[1]

The White Sox really lost the 1919 World Series because they could not hit the Reds' pitching, not because of the failed mound appearances of Cicotte and Williams.

Of all the White Sox hitters in the series the most anemic bat by far belonged to Swede Risberg who hit a near rock bottom .080. At the plate in the series Risberg left nine men on base in scoring position. In the second game lost by the White Sox 4-2, Risberg twice ended rallies in the second and fourth innings by flying out off Slim Sallee. His inability to hit in game two cost the Sox a split of the first two games in Cincinnati.

However, the record should reflect that in the 1919 season, Risberg had only hit .256 with 106 hits in 414 at bats. The fact that Risberg was certainly no slugger limits the argument at best regarding his level of participation in the alleged conspiracy. The fact is that Risberg had a lot of trouble hitting American League pitching, much less the superb pitching of the Cincinnati Reds staff in the World Series.

Furthermore, the fact that Swede Risberg's fielding average in the series was just .930 with four errors is not a huge surprise either. Risberg's regular season fielding average of .934 in 1919 was sixth lowest among the eight starting shortstops in the American League. Swede was a far cry from being an Ozzie Smith ground-ball-eating-machine shortstop. Prior to the start of the 1919 season Kid Gleason had even considered moving Buck Weaver to shortstop and starting Fred McMullin at third, thus confining the weak hitting and poor fielding Risberg to the bench.

As far as character is considered it should be pointed out that rumors about Swede Risberg throwing games and taking bribes began with his rookie season in 1917. Risberg was a tough guy who in one incident following a game was supposed have fought baseball sociopath Ty Cobb to a draw under the grandstand. Shoeless Joe Jackson was to remark later that he was afraid for his life if he alerted anyone to the alleged conspiracy, stating that Risberg had threatened him if he squawked.[2]

The bottom line on Risberg though is that even if he was not involved in a conspiracy, he was not going to produce more on the field then he actually did with the shadow of doubt upon him. Risberg was simply a marginal major leaguer and weak link in the White Sox lineup.

Oscar Emil "Happy" Felsch seemed to have been, for lack of better terms, sucked into something he didn't fully understand. He freely admitted to author Eliot Asinof (*Eight Men Out*) that he "just fell into it" and "I never believed that it would happen." Perhaps Felsch was overconfident and like so many others never believed that it was possible for the Reds to beat the White Sox, conspiracy or not. Felsch later admitted his guilt to a reporter about receiving money from gamblers during the 1919 World Series.

Happy, who batted .275 during the regular season, is yet another case of a White Sox hitter being handicapped by the Reds pitchers as he could only manage to hit .192 in the series.

Felsch apparently developed a taste for the dark side of baseball, however, because it is alleged that he continued to throw games during the 1920 season.

As for nonindicted player Fred McMullin, it does not make a hill of beans to consider if he was an alleged conspirator and in on the fix or not, as he had absolutely no impact on the outcome in any of the games. McMullin appeared in two games, going to bat twice in the series, with one hit for a .500 average. In the field he handled one attempt successfully for a 1.000 average.

Buck Weaver is the most interesting case among the alleged conspirators both by his off-field and on-field alleged levels of participation. Interestingly enough, most conspiracy theory devotees tend to give Weaver a break, some even suggest his innocence. I for one cannot buy the popular theory that Weaver sat in on all the conspiracy meetings with both gamblers and players, but then refused to go along with the scheme.

Weaver was a player who without a doubt could have played in any era with authority. However, it defies logic to accept that he would approach the situation so casually and remain passive while his teammates were blowing games in the World Series, while he was out busting his butt at third base stopping line drives and at bat collecting 11 hits, while hitting .324. However, the record shows that Weaver remained adamant until his death on January 31, 1956, that he knew nothing of a conspiracy to throw the series.

Weaver was either in or out of the alleged fix. Or perhaps the conspiracy was a lot less widespread among the White Sox players than the conspiracy theory advocates have led us to believe over the past 81 years. Perhaps there were actually only five White Sox players—Cicotte, Williams, Risberg, Gandil and Felsch—who were actively participating in the alleged conspiracy. As for Weaver, Jackson and McMullin, there is absolutely no evidence *or strong suggestion of evidence* that they altered their play in the World Series.

That brings us to the alleged involvement of the much-maligned Shoeless Joe Jackson. Jackson batted .375 in the series but is often accused of not hitting when it counted by those convinced of his involvement in the alleged conspiracy. Actually the first one to accuse Jackson of not hitting when it counted was none other than Eddie Cicotte. Yet one hears this diatribe from any conspiracy angler.

To say that Joe Jackson didn't hit when it counted in the series is a charge that has simply become fashionable and is an allegation without foundation.

The reality is that Jackson hit well throughout the series while a non-alleged conspirator like Eddie Collins didn't come alive with the bat until it was too late. Jackson entered game eight with a batting average of .370 and got two hits, one of which was a home run. Now Jackson's home run has been determined useless because he hit it with two out in the bottom of the third. Yet at the same time Eddie Collins entered into the eighth game with a batting average of .140 and got three hits. Well there has never been any criticism of Collins who got three useless hits in the same game that Jackson got two. Again there has always been inconsistency in the conspiracy theory when applied to different players.

However, Jackson wound up in hot water by being implicated in the alleged conspiracy, but he maintained that his only wrongdoing was that he roomed on the road with Claude "Lefty" Williams. Jackson maintained his wrongdoing was guilt by association. In fact when Judge Kenesaw Mountain Landis barred Jackson for life, the reasoning of the commissioner was offered as "for the company you keep."

Despite his earlier grand jury testimony, Joe Jackson later maintained that he played his heart out in the 1919 World Series. If Jackson was dispirited such as Eddie Collins is alleged to have been, his .375 batting average sure didn't show it.

Nonetheless, while Jackson's on-field actions are pretty convincing that he was playing ball for real, his off-field involvement is suspect due to the alleged admission of having received $5,000 from Lefty Williams during his testimony to the grand jury on September 28, 1920. This amount ironically would have been equal to his winning share if the Sox had won the series.

But who can say for sure what was really in Jackson's grand jury testimony. In June 1921 the jury in Cook County (Chicago), Illinois, acquitted all seven of the alleged White Sox conspirators for a lack of evidence. Jackson and the other alleged conspirators recanted their grand jury statements.

Without the testimonies and confessions, the legal issue of an alleged conspiracy to throw games by the eight White Sox players implicated is moot and based entirely on hearsay and circumstantial evidence. Eighty-one years later there is still no evidence of the Sox's plan to lose the series to the Reds. How were the losses to be engineered on the field? What games would be lost? The first, the second, the eighth or even the ninth if needed? There is a lot of speculation about that meeting which took place in Eddie Cicotte's Hotel Sinton room the night before game one in Cincinnati. Who would attempt to do the dirty work on the field? All that is presented as evidence by conspiracy theory devotees time after time is a couple of poor pitching outings by Lefty Williams and a couple of bungled cut-off plays by Eddie Cicotte and Swede Risberg. This does not amount to an all-out, well-planned conspiracy to throw the series. The hard evidence just does not exist.

Furthermore, as previously stated in this work, Reds center fielder Edd Roush, an eyewitness on the field to these events in 1919, truly believed that Cicotte and the other alleged White Sox conspirators may have decided to throw the first game, but then played to the best of their abilities in the remaining seven games.

In the eighth inning of the eighth game, Cincinnati outfielders Greasy Neale and Edd Roush both muffed fly balls that aided a four-run rally by the White Sox. Were the Reds attempting to delay the end of the series? This type of wild speculation is what one hears over and over again as those convinced of the conspiracy grapple with the chore of finding conclusive evidence by the White Sox players' on-the-field play to throw games, while at the same time perpetuating a double standard.

Joe Jackson also muffed a fly ball in the eighth game when in the second inning he misjudged a fly ball hit by Edd Roush and let it sail over his head. However, unlike the miscues of Roush and Neale in the eighth inning of the same game, Jackson's miscue is immediately implicated as intentional and part of a larger scheme to dump the series. Jackson's on-field actions are subject to hasty generalizations by his critics.

This episode, like most evidence presented by the conspiracy theory devotees, is disjointed and not cohesive enough to show a consistent pattern of play that would lead to a definitive conclusion that the White Sox collectively were attempting day in and day out, game by game and play to play to throw the series. The evidence is just not there.

Joe Jackson is really a case of false cause. The twisted logic applied to the off-field and on-field actions of Jackson in an alleged conspiracy is that since he accepted an alleged bribe then it was automatically cause for him to not play to the best of his ability. In short the influence of the first act of accepting an alleged bribe is cause for the second act of lying down, simply because it happened first.

By dismantling the National Commission in 1920 and hiring Judge Landis, Charles Comiskey and the other owners had introduced a corporate culture of apathy into the Major Leagues that led to blind side reasoning being administered to Jackson in the alleged conspiracy. Consequently, with a corporate culture of apathy thoroughly entrenched in the major leagues, the corruption fall-out, rumors and innuendoes from the 1919 World Series continued for years after.

Hal Chase, gambler and former Giants and Reds first baseman, who is thought to have pursued Bill Burns to convince Arnold Rothstein to bankroll the scandal, is believed to have made $40,000 betting on the Reds in the series.

In 1920 it was rumored that the White Sox had dumped the American League pennant to the Cleveland Indians.

In 1926, player managers Ty Cobb of the Detroit Tigers and Tris Speaker of the Cleveland Indians both resigned in a cloud of suspicion after ex-pitcher Dutch Leonard alleged the two had conspired to fix the last game of the 1919 American League season so that the Tigers could win third place money.

To this very day major league baseball has remained absolutely paranoid about keeping gambling elements out of the game.

All time hit king Pete Rose knows this all too well. Rose was known during his playing days to be a gambler and a frequent inhabitant at race tracks in big league cities around the country from Turfway Park across the Ohio River from Cincinnati in Kentucky to Yonkers Raceway right above the Bronx in New York City. Rose is alleged to have placed bets on major league games (including the Reds) while the manager of the Reds in 1988 from the telephone in his clubhouse office in Riverfront Stadium.

Rose like Joe Jackson and the other seven alleged 1919 White Sox conspirators was banned for life from major league baseball in September 1989, by then commissioner A. Bartlett Giamatti.

Current baseball commissioner Bud Selig stated in an interview during early 2000 on New York City radio station WFAN that "Pete Rose will never be reinstated while he is commissioner of baseball." Selig, who has a consistent disregard and ignorance of baseball history, has an agenda in the Rose situation that hurts baseball more than it helps it. Selig will not return calls to Rose and personally puts himself in the position of barring Rose from his rightful place in the Baseball Hall of Fame despite his contributions as a player and the adulation of millions of fans.

This blind-side reasoning exhibited by Selig in the Rose case is absolutely parallel to the prejudicial reasoning applied in the case of Joe Jackson that has occurred with every baseball commissioner from Judge Landis to Happy Chandler to Bowie Kuhn and beyond.

If justice for Rose is not forthcoming in the next few years, then he like Jackson will find his magnificent contributions to baseball on the field and devotion to the game obscured by the myths that will grow in time in regards to his character.

Facts and truths about Pete Rose as a player will become distorted as they did over time with Joe Jackson and his superb play in 1919 World Series. Rose's true achievements in baseball will eventually become secondary to the taint and hype that has resulted from the perpetuation of myths due to his banishment from the game.

But most unfortunate of all for Pete Rose is that his rightful place in baseball's sacred shrine, the Hall of Fame, will be denied as a result of a small man like Bud Selig who fantasizes that somehow as he has achieved the office of Commissioner of Baseball then he must be at the same level of integrity and stature as Judge Kenesaw Mountain Landis. Therefore, Pete Rose is his Joe Jackson and his ultimate legacy in the office.

When Ted Williams joined the Boston Red Sox as a rookie in 1939, Eddie Collins was a member of the Red Sox executive staff. In 1999 Williams said, "Collins told him that Joe Jackson was not in on the fix during the 1919 World Series." Consequently, Williams, Bob Feller and Hank Aaron have been soliciting support to have Jackson's name cleared in the scandal and have him admitted to the Baseball Hall of Fame in Cooperstown, New York.

One of the most incredible fallacies of the 1919 World Series that is advanced by the conspiracy theorists is that the White Sox pitchers, mainly Cicotte and Williams, were going to blow the Reds batters away. Well the fact of the matter is that the Reds were routinely used to facing very good pitchers in the National League. Grover Cleveland Alexander, Hippo Vaughn and Fred Toney all had lower ERAs in 1919 than Lefty Williams and in fact both Alexander and Vaughn had lower ERAs than Cicotte.

The reality of the White Sox pitching in the series was it was severely hampered by the fact that pitcher Red Faber was out of the World Series because he was either disabled or sick, or both. Consequently, the White Sox had to face the Reds in a nine-game series with three starting pitchers.

The facts surrounding the events of the 1919 World Series have become extremely distorted over the years. Now there are even conflicting views on the nature of Faber's disability. One theory is that he had the flu. Another has it that Faber had a sore arm and couldn't pitch. Yet another story often heard is that Red Faber missed the 1919 World Series because of a sore ankle.

Whatever, Urban "Red" Faber was a money pitcher who was the White Sox hero of the 1917 World Series in which he had won three games for the Sox over the Giants. In that same series Eddie Cicotte could only win one game, while Lefty Williams could win none.

Cicotte, the White Sox ace, had been pitching bad games the last couple of weeks of the 1919 season. The wear and tear of his 35 starts in a 140-game season was taking a toll on his arm. In fact Cicotte had started 25 percent of the White Sox games in 1919.

The Reds on the other hand had six starting pitchers to use: Dutch Ruether, Slim Sallee, Ray Fisher, Jimmy Ring, Hod Eller and Dolf Luque.

The Reds pitchers finished the 1919 World Series with a 1.69 ERA, throwing two shutouts and allowing only 55 hits in eight games (6.8 hits per game). Of the 32 teams that had played in the World Series from 1903 through 1919, the Reds pitching staff had achieved the seventh lowest team ERA in World Series history at that point in time.

Furthermore, the White Sox had to employ their meager pitching staff against a Reds team that had the second best team batting average of .261 in the National League. The result was that the Reds outscored the White Sox 35-20 in the series. Just considering the inequities of the available pitching between the White Sox and Reds is cause enough to argue emphatically that there was no way that Chicago was going to win the 1919 World Series.

If it had not been for the unprecedented pitching of a rookie, Dickie Kerr, the series would have been over in five straight games.

Notwithstanding Kerr's heroics in game three, the series would have still been over in six games if it were not for two Cincinnati players, left fielder Pat Duncan and shortstop Larry Kopf, that stood and watched a lazy fly ball hit the ground between them in the top of the sixth inning that started a big White Sox rally in game six.

Then later in the game Reds manager Pat Moran sent a pitcher up to bat who couldn't hit. With two men on and two outs in the bottom of the eighth, Moran should have pinch-hit for weak hitting pitcher Jimmy Ring. Sitting on the Reds bench available for pinch-hitting duties in the bottom of the eighth was none other than Sherry Magee, a right-handed batter who in his 16-year big league career had won two National League batting crowns and had gotten 2,169 hits. Sending Jimmy Ring up to hit in the bottom eighth was a colossal blunder and probably delayed the end of the series and the ultimate Cincinnati championship.

If somehow despite the fact that Lefty Williams was pulverized by the Reds' bats in game eight, the White Sox would have come back and won the game sending the series to a deciding ninth game, then Dickie Kerr would have had to face the Reds on two days rest. Whether Kerr would have been up to the task is at least debatable.

The Reds on the other hand could have started either Jimmy Ring, who had five days rest, or Ray Fisher, who had six days rest between starts, or a well-rested Dutch Ruether. It simply wasn't in the cards for the White Sox to win the series without having Red Faber available to pitch in the rotation, conspiracy or not.

Another key fact in the White Sox loss in the series that is almost never mentioned in advancing the conspiracy notion is that nonalleged conspirator Eddie "Cocky" Collins, who had batted a robust .319 during the regular season, batted only .226 with just one extra-base hit facing the Reds' brilliant pitching in the World Series. To say that Collins' performance was a huge let down to the White Sox's efforts is an understatement.

Yet there are some baseball historians who have the outrageous audacity to argue that Eddie Collins' poor performance in the 1919 World Series was simply the result of his being dispirited by some of his teammates' play or lack of it.

Nonetheless, any way that you want to cut it the fact remains that Collins, who was the White Sox third leading RBI man in the 1919 season with 80 RBIs behind Joe Jackson's 96 and Happy Felsch's 86, was so overwhelmed by the Reds' sharp pitching in the series that he did not get his first and only RBI of the series until the sixth game when the Reds then held a 4-1 advantage and had the White Sox on the verge of elimination.

It's high time for history to finally assign a huge portion of the necessary blame for the Chicago White Sox defeat in the 1919 World Series to Eddie Collins. His weak performance at the plate was just as devastating to the Sox as any base on balls issued by Lefty Williams in games two or five, or Chick Gandil's alleged waltz down the base paths in the third game. Hall of Famer Eddie Collins was a complete bust for the White Sox in the

1919 World Series and the team suffered a defeat in the World Series because of it.

One can be fair to Eddie Collins; everyone just cannot be Mr. October (Reggie Jackson, batting average of .357 for 27 games) when it comes to hitting in the World Series. In reality good players as well as great players have a lousy World Series with the bat every year. It happens all the time, every October, but their teams usually suffer as a result of their weak hitting and blame due is historically assigned.

Ted Williams in 1946, in his only World Series appearance, batted a lowly .200 and the Cardinals defeated the Red Sox. But no one implied that World Series was rigged because Williams failed to hit.

Even the fence-busting Babe Ruth, the "Bambino," "the sultan of swat," was a bust with the bat in a World Series! In 1922 Babe Ruth hit a paltry .118 in the World Series and the Giants swept the Yankees in four games.

Dick Sisler, who hit the home run that won the pennant for the Philadelphia Phillies Whiz Kids in their 1950 playoff game with the Dodgers, batted a paltry .059 in the World Series that year as the Yankees took the series in four straight games.

More recently Mark McGwire hit a robust .059 in the 1988 World Series that saw the Dodgers defeat the Oakland A's 4-1.

The failure of Collins to hit in the 1919 World Series must be figured into the total equation of the White Sox's loss in the series right alongside those ten suspicious plays that make up the conspiracy theory.

Collins aside, the failure of the White Sox team to hit in the series, having achieved the 17th lowest batting average in World Series history at that time, was only paled in comparison by the team's poor showing on the mound. The White Sox hurlers with a team ERA of 3.68 had achieved the third highest ERA in World Series history at that time among the 32 teams that had previously played in the fall classic.

Conspiracy theorists constantly and without foundation shift the mood of the conspiracy to accommodate their need to answer why the actual events occurred. A popular theory shared by many conspiracy junkies is that when the White Sox players did not receive the $40,000 in cash from the gamblers after dropping the first two games of the series in Cincinnati, they felt betrayed and began to lose interest in the conspiracy. Subsequently, after gamblers did not pay an additional $20,000 to the players following their loss in game five in Chicago, on the train ride back to Cincinnati for game six with the White Sox facing elimination in the series 4-1, the players evidently decided to abandon their plot and play the series straight. Well it is true that Lefty Williams did testify to that account in the case of Cicotte and before the grand jury.

But this incident is often exaggerated in advancing the conspiracy theory by oversimplifying the notion that the mighty 1919 White Sox, the so called "greatest team ever assembled," grew tired of the conspiracy and therefore kicked into high gear and won games six and seven in Cincinnati sending the series back to Chicago by narrowing the Reds' seemingly insurmountable lead of 4-1 to now just 4-3.

How extraordinary for the devotees of the conspiracy theory and of those White Sox fans that support the team superiority myth alike to travel out on the extreme boundaries of analysis to search for answers in the justification for the alleged conspiracy turnaround by questioning the team's mental health and speculating on the mood swings of the players.

The spin here is very clear though. When the White Sox are losing games in the 1919 World Series, the fix is in. However, when the White Sox are suddenly winning games, it is because this great team is now playing ball for real. There are no other words to describe this type of speculation, what a farce!

However, the most popular theory of the alleged conspiracy is that all eight of the White Sox players implicated remained steadfast to the end in their desire to throw the series to the Reds. But the play by play record describing the team's action does not show consistent evidence of players attempting to dump ball games throughout the series.

Whatever chicanery that may have been plotted by Chick Gandil and discussed in Eddie Cicotte's Hotel Sinton room the night before the series began came crashing down in the reality of the Reds' ambush and gritty determined play in the moments following Cicotte's second pitch in game one that smacked into the back of Morrie Rath. The fact of the matter is that the Reds ran away with game one of the series and never looked back. At that point the 1919 World Series was for all intensive purposes over.

The White Sox were outhit and outpitched by the Reds. For conspiracy theory advocates to say that Joe Jackson didn't hit when it counted is a gross generalization. The entire White Sox team did not hit when it counted. In the eight games of the series the White Sox left a total of 48 men on base in scoring position (second or third base). In game two in which the White Sox lost to the Reds 4-2, they left eight men on base in scoring position. Even in game eight they left seven men on base in scoring position. The Reds pitchers just would not let the White Sox score when they needed it most. Their inability to score had little to do with the alleged untimely hitting of Joe Jackson.

If it had not been for White Sox catcher Ray Schalk, who time and time again cut down Reds runners attempting to steal second base, the winning scores produced by the Reds in most of the games would have been totally lopsided. The White Sox were beaten and beaten thoroughly in the series.

On October 9, 1919, following game eight and Cincinnati's victory in the World Series, Jim Nasium wrote in his column for the *Philadelphia Inquirer*.

> The World's title is theirs this evening by a margin of five games to three and the best baseball club won. The Reds have simply outclassed the White Sox all through the series, richly deserving the honors that are now theirs and in no game did they so clearly display their superiority as they did in the curtain engagement here this afternoon.
>
> Those experts who were so fond of comparing the opposing players on the two teams on a basis shown by the official averages of the past season, may now take a slant at the comparisons that were displayed when the two teams met in actual conflict in the series that closed here today.
>
> Though the advance dope based on official averages of the playing season showed that the White Sox by far out classed the Reds in individual comparison, in this series they have shown superiority in only one position — John (Shano) Collins and Leibold having a shade on the playing of Neale in right field. John Collins who had not been considered as one of the White Sox stars played by far the best and most consistent ball of any or both at bat and in the field.
>
> In the other positions Pat Duncan, the youth who broke into the series fresh from the Southern League, had it all over Joe Jackson. Eddie Roush made Felsch look like a sandlotter. Larry Kopf had it all over Risberg. Jake Daubert made Chick Gandil look like the rankest busher, while Ivy Wingo and Bill Rariden outcaught Schalk, star catcher of the American League, by a mile or more. In addition the Reds pitching staff outpitched Gleason's.
>
> The only positions in which the Sox held the Reds to a tie in the individual comparison was at third base and second where Buck Weaver and Eddie Collins played about a standoff against Groh and Morris Rath, but they were no better than the pair of Reds.
>
> Now then how can anybody alibi a ball club that has been so clearly outplayed individually and then has in addition displayed such poor generalship and absolutely no fighting force or guts. The Reds are champions of the great, throbbing world of baseball tonight because they deserve to be. They went into this fight with the determination and competitive spirit that marks all good champions. Our hat is off to the Cincinnati Reds.

I am convinced that against the White Sox in the 1919 World Series, with or without a taint of an alleged conspiracy, the Reds would have won anyway and won in less than eight games too. I will just never be convinced that the 1919 Chicago White Sox, while a good team, were not any better competition for the Reds than those they confronted during the regular season while facing the New York Giants and Chicago Cubs.

The conspiracy theory in the 1919 World Series continues to exist because it is what a majority of people want to believe.

It is apparent just how endemic this mindset is when you consider how much emphasis is placed on the pitching of Dickie Kerr and how little emphasis is placed on the pitching of Hod Eller, Jimmy Ring or Adolpho Luque. Or when you consider how much emphasis is placed on errors of Eddie Cicotte and how little emphasis is placed on the great fielding of Edd Roush.

On and on it goes. A common thread through every book, every news article, every video, every movie, every sports talk radio show. Always a protracted dialogue on the suspect plays of the White Sox in every game and no mention of the superb play of the Reds in any game.

The stream of misinformation in regard to the 1919 World Series is so casually accepted that time after time in media of all forms one notices the most common mistake of journalist, sportswriters, sportscasters and the average sports fan alike, who repeatedly state that "*eight* White Sox players were *convicted* of throwing the series." It simply begs the question, will they ever get it right?

Well, probably not.

While the off-field case against Cicotte, Gandil and Williams may have merit; the on-field case against all seven players indicted is at most hair-splitting.

Even the grand jury hearing was suspect in establishing the facts of a conspiracy. The prosecutors could not call necessary witnesses such as Abe Attell, Billy Burns, Bill Maharg or even Arnold Rothstein because they were tainted witnesses with no credibility. Instead the prosecutors relied on coerced confessions of a few ball players who had been intimidated.

In a court of law a person is presumed innocent until proven guilty, yet the owners such as Charles Comiskey and prosecutors alike did little to arrive at the truth in the alleged conspiracy, but rather appealed to pity for the sake of getting their conclusion that the series was fixed accepted. Bribes rather than actual play on the field took center stage in the indictments, leaving evidence and questions of the law swept aside in the rush to judgment.

Nonetheless, it's high time and very long overdue for all the baseball fans, historians and writers to take a new look at the 1919 World Series and stop focusing on the conspiracy angle and begin to focus on the hustle of the World Champion Cincinnati Reds. The Reds were not in awe of the Chicago White Sox as the legend has it. Rather they bristled with confidence in the 1919 World Series as evidenced by their constant taunt-ing of the White Sox and their relentless, determined slick play on the field. Can anyone argue that justice delayed is indeed justice denied? After 81 years it is time to finally give the 1919 Cincinnati Reds the respect that they have so deserved in baseball history. The best team won.

CHAPTER THIRTEEN

Beyond 1919: Whatever Happened to the Players, Managers, Owners and Teams

Below are brief experiences of various events that followed in the lives of the Reds and White Sox players, managers, owners and franchises following the incredible drama of the 1919 World Series, the 1920 season and the subsequent acquittal of the accused eight White Sox players in 1921.

Players, Cincinnati Reds

Rube Bressler—He came up to the majors with Connie Mack's Philadelphia Athletics in 1914 as a pitcher and had a record of 10-4. After being returned to the minors he was picked up by the Reds in 1917. He did not make an appearance in the 1919 World Series. That season Rube was in transition of becoming an outfielder after being a pitcher for several years. In 1920 he would pitch in ten games, appear as in outfielder in three and play first base in two others. However, by 1921 the transition would become complete and Bressler would hit .307, playing in 109 games for the Reds. He would do even better in the 1924 season when he would hit .347 in 115 games.

Then on March 13, 1928, the Reds sold Rube to Brooklyn for the waiver price and his career took off. The next three seasons he would be a regular in the Dodger outfield and never hit lower than .295. He finished his 19-year major league career with the Philadelphia Phillies and St. Louis Cardinals in 1932. As a pitcher Rube had a career record of 26-32 with an ERA of 3.40. As a converted outfielder he had a career batting average of .301 with 1,170 hits. During his career he would have the distinction of having three future Hall of Fame members as roommates, Chief Bender, Eppa Rixey and Dazzy Vance. He died on November 7, 1966, in the Cincinnati neighborhood of Mt. Washington.

Jake Daubert— A player forgotten by time that should have been enshrined in Cooperstown by now. He played out the remainder of his brilliant 15-year major league career with the Reds. Daubert, who had won two National League batting titles with the Brooklyn Dodgers (1913 and 1914) prior to being traded to Cincinnati in March 1919 in exchange for Tommy Griffith, ended his career with a .303 batting average and 2,326 hits. In 1914 he had won the Chalmers Most Valuable Player Award (the forerunner of today's MVP award that was only in effect for four years 1911–1914). Jake died just a few weeks after the 1924 season was concluded on October 9 in Cincinnati.

Pat Duncan— In 1921 Pat became the first player to ever hit a home run out of Redland Field. His blast cleared the left field wall and hit an unsuspecting policeman standing in York Street. He concluded his seven-year major league career with the Reds in 1924 with a .307 lifetime average and 827 hits. He died on July 17, 1960, in Jackson, Ohio.

Horace "Hod" Eller— Following his 20-9 record in 1919, Hod was 13-12 in 1920. He played his entire five-year major league career with the Reds. Following the 1921 season he retired with a lifetime record of 61-40. Eller died on July 18, 1961, in Indianapolis.

Ray Fisher— He had come to the Reds on waivers after spending 1918 in the U.S. Army. Fisher concluded his ten-year big league career (8 years New York Giants and 2 years Reds) in 1920 with a 10-11 record for Cincinnati. Lifetime Fisher was 100-94 with an ERA of 2.82.

Following the 1920 season the Reds wanted to cut his salary by $1,000. Rather than accept the cut he requested his release from the Reds, then accepted an offer to become the baseball coach and freshman football coach at the University of Michigan. For requesting his release he was banned for life from major league baseball by Commissioner Judge Kenesaw Mountain Landis. Nonetheless, Fisher went on to coach for 38 years at Michigan and win nine Big Ten Championships in baseball. One of the freshman football players coached by Fisher at Michigan was Gerald R. Ford (38th president of the United States, 1974–77). Fisher died on November 3,

1962, at 95 in Ann Arbor, Michigan. In 1980 Commissioner Bowie Kuhn reinstated Fisher as a player in good standing with major league baseball.

Ed "Lefty" Gerner— The young southpaw who had started just one game for the Reds in 1919 and that wanted the chance to face the White Sox in game six never played in the big leagues again following the 1919 season. His career record was 1-0 with an ERA of 3.18 for 17 innings. Gerner died on May 15, 1970, in Philadelphia.

Heinie Groh— He played two more seasons in Cincinnati, hitting .298 in 1920 and .331 in 1921. Following the 1921 season Heinie was traded by the Reds to the New York Giants on December 6, 1921, for Mike Gonzalez, George Burns and $150,000 in cash.

In the 1922 World Series he hit .474 as the Giants swept the Yankees 4-0. He would conclude his 16-year major league career by playing in 14 games for the National League Champion Pittsburgh Pirates in 1927. He made just one appearance in the 1927 World Series, pinch-hitting without making a hit.

He used his famous bottle bat to hammer out 1,774 hits in his career with a .292 batting average. Groh then remained in baseball managing in the minor leagues and scouting for the Giants, Dodgers and Phillies. He died on August 22, 1968, in Cincinnati.

Larry Kopf— He had played five games for the 1913 Cleveland Indians under the name of Fred Brady. A World War I veteran prior to joining the Reds for the 1919 season, he played two more seasons in Cincinnati. On February 18, 1922, he was traded to the Boston Braves. He had a lifetime batting average of .249 and played for ten years in the big leagues. Larry died shortly before his 96th birthday on October 15, 1986, in Hamilton County, Ohio.

Dolf Luque— Known as "The Pride of Havana," he was one of the first native Cuban ball players to become a star in the major leagues. Following the 1919 series Dolf continued to pitch ten more years for the Reds. After compiling a 13-23 record in 1921, Dolf turned it all around and had an amazing season in 1922 with a 27-8 record. He led the National League in wins (27), winning percentage (.771), ERA (1.93) and shutouts (6).

In February 1930 the Reds traded him to the Brooklyn Dodgers for Doug McWeeny. He then pitched two years in Brooklyn before concluding his 20-year big league career with the New York Giants (1932–1935).

In the 1933 World Series Luque, now 43 years old, made a relief appearance in the fifth game against the Washington Senators pitching 4⅓ innings without allowing a run. His lifetime record was 193-179. Dolf died in Havana, Cuba, on July 3, 1957.

Sherry Magee— The 1919 World Series was the end of the line for

Magee who was completing a brilliant 16-year major league career with the Philadelphia Phillies, 1904–1914, Boston Braves, 1915–1917, and the Reds, 1917–1919. He had played in 2,085 games and finished with a .291 batting average and 2,169 hits. In 1910 he had led the National League in hitting with a .331 average and led the league in RBIs in 1910 and 1915. He turned to umpiring after his playing career ended and spent one season as a National League umpire before he died from complications associated with pneumonia on March 13, 1929, in Philadelphia.

Earle "Greasy" Neale— Following his great performance in the 1919 World Series in which he led the Reds in hitting with a .357 average and 13 total bases, he continued to play with Cincinnati until being traded to the Philadelphia Phillies along with pitcher Jimmy Ring on February 22, 1921, in exchange for future Hall of Fame pitcher Eppa Rixey. Ironically on June 2, 1921, after playing in just 22 games for the Phillies, he was sold back to the Reds for the waiver price. He then finished his baseball career with the Reds, playing through the 1924 season.

His big league statistics for eight years included a lifetime batting average of .259 and 688 hits. Known for his speed, he had a career total 139 stolen bases.

In the off-season during his baseball playing days, he had played football professionally and coached at the college level as well. After leaving baseball, Alfred Earle "Greasy" Neale turned full-time to football.

In 1940 Neale was hired as coach of the Philadelphia Eagles in the NFL. Under Neale's leadership the Eagles won the NFL Eastern title in 1947, but lost the championship game to the Chicago Cardinals 28-21. However, the following season Neale's Eagles returned to the NFL championship game and beat the Chicago Cardinals 7-0. In 1949 the Eagles under Neale's coaching finished the season 11-1 then defeated the Los Angeles Rams 14-0 in their third consecutive NFL championship game. Neale was eventually elected into the Pro Football Hall of Fame. Greasy Neale died on November 2, 1973, in Lake Worth, Florida.

Bill Rariden— In 1920 he played one more season for the Reds, playing in 39 games and hitting .248, while wrapping up a 12-year major league career.

Of course Rariden will always be known for being part of one of the most infamous plays in World Series history. In the sixth game of the 1917 World Series between the White Sox and Giants, Rariden was behind the plate when Eddie Collins broke from third on a taper back to the mound by Happy Felsch. Giants pitcher Rube Benton tossed the ball to Heinie Zimmerman at third. However, Rariden had moved up the third base line and Collins just blew by him, leaving the plate unprotected and with Giant third sacker Zimmerman in hot pursuit, chasing Collins across the plate. Rariden died on August 28, 1942, in Bedford, Indiana.

Morrie Rath— He concluded his six-year major league career by playing one more season for the Reds in 1920, hitting .267 for 506 trips to the plate in 129 games. He was one of four players to play in a tripleheader in the modern era. He played in this tripleheader on his last day in the big leagues on October 2, 1920.

In 1912 and 1913 Morrie had been the White Sox regular second baseman. Prior to coming to the Reds he played in the minors and served in the U.S. Navy in World War I. He died on November 18, 1945, in Upper Darby, Pennsylvania.

Jimmy Ring— He played one more season with Cincinnati in 1920 going 17-16 with an ERA of 3.23. On February 22, 1921, the Reds traded Ring along with Greasy Neale to the Philadelphia Phillies for future Hall of Fame pitcher Eppa Rixey. In 1923 he won 18 games for the last place Phillies.

However, Ring, always known for his hard throwing as well as his wildness, led National League pitchers in walks from 1922 through 1925.

After spending five seasons with the Phillies, on December 30, 1925, he was traded to the New York Giants in exchange for Jack Bentley and Wayland Dean. He played one season for the Giants in 1926 compiling a record of 11-10. On December 20, 1926, he was traded by the Giants along with future Hall of Fame member Frankie Frisch to the St. Louis Cardinals in exchange for future Hall of Fame member Rogers Hornsby. The following December he was traded for the third year in a row, this time back to the Phillies where he concluded his 12-year major league career going 4-17. Lifetime Ring was 118-149 with an ERA of 4.06. He died on July 6, 1965, in New York City.

Edd Roush— After being traded to the Reds by the New York Giants in 1916, he won two National League batting crowns (1917 and 1919). The trade that brought Roush to the Reds remains an enigma among baseball trivia buffs, as it is the only trade that ever included three future Hall of Fame members. On July 20, 1916, the Giants traded future Hall of Fame members Roush, Christy Mathewson and Bill McKechnie to the Reds for Buck Herzog and Red Killefer.

Following the 1919 series Edd continued to play for the Reds seven more seasons and in each year he hit over .300. In fact he hit over .300 for 11 straight seasons (1917–1927) and never hit under .321 in a season during the period of 1917 to 1926. Despite the superior efforts of Roush, the Reds did not win another pennant between 1920 and 1926.

On February 9, 1927, he was traded back to the New York Giants for George Kelly and cash. Roush was reluctant to return to the Giants and play for John McGraw, who he personally despised. According to Roush, McGraw had an abrasive demeanor and belittled his players, often calling them every name in the book. When accord was reached in finding a way to blend the fierce personalities of Roush and McGraw, he then agreed to the trade that also included a $70,000 three-year contract.

In 1927 he hit .304 with 173 hits for the Giants. Following the end of his three-year contract with the Giants, Edd returned to play one more season with the Reds in 1931. In that season he batted just .271 in 101 games. The following year he retired after spending 18 years in the major leagues with a career batting mark of .323 and collecting 2,376 hits.

Roush saved his money and invested it wisely. Subsequently, he had a very comfortable retirement. Being without question one of the National League's all-time finest outfielders, in 1962 Roush was elected to the Baseball Hall of Fame in Cooperstown along with a class that included Jackie Robinson, Bob Feller and Bill McKechnie. Also that year he was selected by the Cincinnati fans as the greatest living Red. He died at the age of 94 on March 21, 1988. Until the day he died Roush maintained the Reds' superiority over the White Sox in the 1919 World Series.

Walter "Dutch" Ruether— He returned to pitch for the Reds in 1920 going 16-12. Dutch, who had hit .667 in the 1919 World Series, continued with his hot bat through the 1920 season with the Reds when he hit .351 (34 for 97).

On December 15, 1920, he was traded to the Brooklyn Dodgers for future Hall of Fame pitcher Rube Marquard. In 1924 the Dodgers sent Dutch to the Washington Senators in exchange for cash. Finally on August 27, 1926, with the New York Yankees heading into a pennant stretch run with the Cleveland Indians, the Senators traded Ruether to the Yankees. Coming down the stretch Dutch was 2-3 for the Yankees. He then made a disastrous starting appearance in game three of the 1926 World Series when the Cardinals broke open the game with three runs off Ruether in the fourth on their way to a 4-0 victory. In all he gave up seven hits in 4⅓ innings with an ERA of 8.31 in his only 1926 series appearance. He then concluded his 11-year major league career with the New York Yankees in 1927. He had a career record of 137-95 with an ERA of 3.50. On May 16, 1970, he died in Phoenix, Arizona.

Harry "Slim" Sallee— The man who got his nickname for carrying 180 pounds on his 6'3" frame returned to pitch part of the 1920 season for the Reds before being sold on waivers September 5, 1920, to the New York Giants. He would pitch one more year in the big leagues for the Giants in 1921 going 6-4. He then retired after 14 seasons with a lifetime record of 173-143 and an ERA of 2.56.

His victory in game two of the 1919 World Series was sweet revenge, for he had previously been beaten by the White Sox twice in the 1917 World Series while with the Giants. In game one of the 1917 series Slim lost a squeaker 2-1 to the White Sox on a fourth inning home run by Happy Felsch. He was then beaten again by the White Sox in game five 8-5. Slim died on March 22, 1950, in Higginsport, Ohio.

Jimmy Smith— A utility player, he was not on a big league roster for the 1920 season. However, on June 28, 1921, the Reds sold him for cash to the Philadelphia Phillies. This was the seventh time since 1915 that Smith had either been traded or sold by major league clubs. He concluded his major league career in 1922 with the Phillies. Lifetime he hit .219 with 247 hits in 370 games. Smith died on January 1, 1974, in Pittsburgh.

Ivy Wingo— He continued to play for the Reds through the 1929 season. In all he played 13 of his 17 years in the major leagues with the Reds and had been the player/manager of the team in 1916. Ivy's lifetime batting average was .260 and he had 1,039 hits in 1,326 games. He died on March 1, 1941, in Norcross, Georgia.

Manager, Cincinnati Reds

Pat Moran— He had seen 14 years service in the National League as a catcher for Boston, Chicago and Philadelphia, 1901–1914. He became manager of the Phillies in 1915 and won a pennant his first year. He then won a pennant in his first year with Cincinnati in 1919 and continued to manage the Reds through the 1923 season until his premature death at the age of 48 on March 7, 1924, in Orlando, Florida. In 9 years as a big league manager he won 748 games and lost 586 for a winning percentage of .561, along with a World Championship in 1919. Only twice did a club Pat managed finish lower than third place. Moran was another that held until his death that the 1919 Reds were a superior team to the 1919 White Sox.

Owner, Cincinnati Reds

August Gary Herrmann— He was nicknamed Garibaldi due to his resemblance when wearing his long tailed brass button coat. Gary was a true major league baseball pioneer who, along with fellow National Commission member and American League President Ban Johnson, is credited with creating the modern World Series. After the National Commission was dissolved in 1921 he continued to be active in the game.

A minority owner in the triumvirate who owned the Reds that included Cincinnati Republican political machine boss George B. Cox and members of the Fleischmann family (Julius and Max) of the yeast industry fame, he remained president of the Reds until 1927. It was under Herrmann's vision that the new Redland Field, with the largest playing area in the major leagues at that time, was constructed in 1911 and dedicated on May 18, 1912. His proudest achievement though was the Reds' 1919 World Series victory over the Chicago White Sox. After being ill for several years, Herrmann died in 1931 at Cincinnati.

Team, Cincinnati Reds

Following the 1919 World Championship, the Cincinnati Reds finished in third place in 1920, 10½ games behind the pennant winning Brooklyn Robins (Dodgers). They had been leading the league entering September, but suddenly hit a tailspin and failed to repeat as pennant winners. Had the Reds repeated as National League champs in 1920, the stigma attached by the conspiracy in the 1919 World Series would have had far less support over the ensuing years in challenging their legitimacy as outright winners of the series.

In 1927 with the resignation of August Gary Herrmann as president, the controlling interest in the Reds was sold to Cincinnati businessman Sidney Weil (an undertaker by trade). However, in October 1929 Weil lost his personal fortune in the stock market crash. Weil's stock in the Reds was then held by the Central Trust Company.

In 1933 the Central Trust Company took over complete control of the Reds and hired Larry MacPhail on the recommendation of Branch Rickey to run the day-to-day operations. In 1934 MacPhail convinced local industrialist Powell Crosley, Jr., to invest in the Reds. By 1936 MacPhail, spending freely, had rebuilt the team and Crosley had become majority owner. Subsequently, the name of Redland Field was changed to Crosley Field. However, MacPhail, a brilliant but boisterous individual and heavy drinker, quit after getting drunk and punching out Crosley in 1937.

Powell Crosley, Jr., was a superior innovator who personally broadcast the first Reds game ever heard on radio. Also he and McPhail introduced night baseball to the major leagues on July 31, 1935, when the Reds hosted the St. Louis Cardinals' infamous "Gas House Gang" (Dizzy and Paul Dean, Pepper Martin, Leo Durocher, Frankie Frisch, Joe "Ducky" Medwick, etc.) in the first night game ever played. For the first night game 30,000 fans were in attendance and a total of 130,337 attended the seven night game schedule for the year. The total attendance figure for those seven night games exceeded the total attendance of some major league clubs in 1935 for their entire 77 home games schedule.

In the late 1930s Crosley Field was expanded with a double deck grandstand. On June 11, 1938, Reds fire-balling left hander Johnny Vander Meer pitched a 3-0 no-hitter against the Boston Braves at Crosley Field. Then four days later in the first night game ever played at Brooklyn's Ebbets Field, Vander Meer would throw his second consecutive no-hit game against the Dodgers.

In 1939 and 1940 the Reds would win back to back National League Championships under the helm of Hall of Fame manager Bill McKechnie. The 1939 and 1940 Reds were led by Hall of Fame catcher Ernie Lombardi and pitching aces Bucky Walters and Paul Derringer. In the 1939 World Series the Reds lost to the New York Yankees 4-0 as Yankee outfielders Charlie Keller hit .438 and Joe DiMaggio .313. However, in 1940 the Reds once again became World Champions defeating the Detroit Tigers in a seven-game series 4-3, despite the fine hitting of Hank Greenberg (.357). Paul Derringer (2-1, 2.79) and Bucky Walters (2-0, 1.50) provided the Reds with some superior pitching in the 1940 World Series.

During the middle 1950s, with the Cold War and anti-Communist frenzy at its peak, the Cincinnati Reds, wishing to disassociate themselves from any possible misrepresentation of their team name, changed the club's name of 62 years from the Reds to Redlegs. This self-imposed paranoia remained in effect from 1953 through 1958.

The 1956 Reds came within a hair of winning the pennant, finishing in third place one game behind the second place Milwaukee Braves and just two games behind the first place Brooklyn Dodgers. The 1956 Reds tied a major league record with 221 home runs led by rookie Frank Robinson with 39 home runs. Wally Post had 36 home runs, big Ted Kluszewski 35, Gus Bell 29 and catcher Ed Bailey 28.

In 1959 the name of the team was changed back to the Reds.

Powell Crosley, Jr., died shortly before the 1961 season began and the team was placed in a trust. The Reds, wearing black armbands on their uniforms to honor Crosley, would win their fourth National League pennant in 1961 led by Hall of Fame outfielder Frank Robinson. However, they would lose the World Series to the New York Yankees 4-1. The fifth and final game played on October 9, 1961, was to be the last World Series game played in Crosley Field.

Although provisions in the trust that Crosley had established stated that controlling interest in the Reds should remain in the Crosley family, a few years later the Reds were sold to General manager Bill DeWitt.

DeWitt threatened to move the Reds to San Diego if a new stadium was not built out in the Cincinnati northern suburban community of Blue Ash, near U.S. Interstate Highway 75. However, in 1967 DeWitt instead sold the ball club for $7 million to a group of local investors that was headed up by *Cincinnati Enquirer* President and Publisher Francis Dale, who called themselves 617, Inc. (the street address of the *Cincinnati Enquirer* at that time, 617 Vine Street).

The final game played at Crosley Field (old Redland Field) took place on June 24, 1970, with the "Big Red Machine" (Pete Rose, Johnny Bench, Tony Perez, etc.) beating the San Francisco Giants 5-4. The old ballpark was demolished in 1972.

The Reds then moved to Riverfront Stadium, their new ballpark located on the Ohio River bank in Cincinnati. The first game would be played at Riverfront Stadium on June 30, 1970, versus the Atlanta Braves to a record crowd of 51,051. Playing in Riverfront Stadium the Reds would win National League pennants in 1970, 1972, 1975, 1976, 1990 and also NL Western Division Championships in 1973 and 1979.

By 1972 Joe Morgan, Cesar Geronimo and Davey Concepcion had joined the Reds and Ken Griffey, Sr., became a full-time player in 1973 thereby rounding out the "Big Red Machine" with Bench, Rose and Perez. In 1975, in order to make room for George Foster in the lineup, Pete Rose would switch positions from left field to third base. Now with one of the most powerful lineups in baseball history, the Reds would win back-to-back World Championships in 1975 and 1976.

In 1975 the Reds defeated the Boston Red Sox 4-3 in a series that most baseball experts agree to as one of the most exciting of all time. In 1976 the "Big Red Machine" first swept the Philadelphia Phillies in the National League Championship series three games to none, then in the World Series swept the New York Yankees 4-0.

The Reds continued to go through a series of ownerships that included local financiers the Williams brothers (Bill and Jim) along with several minority shareholders. On December 21, 1984, the Williams brothers sold their controlling interest in the Reds to local car dealership magnate Marge Unnewehr Schott for about $9 million. Minority interests included, Louis Nippert, Frisch's Restaurants, Inc., Priscilla Gamble, Chicago book dealer Carl Kroch (Kroch & Bertinos) and Cincinnati businessman George Strike.

In 1990 the Reds would win a World Championship by sweeping the powerful Oakland A's led by the "bash brothers" José Canseco and Mark McGwire, 4-0. The 1990 Reds were led by shortstop Barry Larkin, outfielders Paul O'Neill and Eric Davis along with a trio of hard throwing relievers Norm Charlton, Rob Dibble and Randy Myers, who referred to themselves as "The Nasty Boys."

In 1993 Marge Schott would be suspended from major league baseball for one year due to a series of insensitive racial remarks made in private that became public. Schott would eventually be forced out of baseball by other major-league owners led by Milwaukee Brewers owner (now commissioner) Bud Selig.

Subsequently the Reds were sold in the late 1990s to another Cincinnati financier Carl Lindner (controlling interest in Chiquita Brands International, Inc., and Amtrak).

In 1994 major league baseball restructured the leagues into three divisions each. The Reds were leading the National League Central Division in August when the players' strike canceled the remainder of the season. However, the Reds won the Central Division Championship in 1995 only to lose in the playoffs to the Western Division Champion Los Angeles Dodgers 3-0.

On March 19, 1996, the voters of Cincinnati authorized a one-half cent sales tax increase for the purpose of raising $544 million to provide funding for two new stadiums on the riverfront. One stadium would house the Cincinnati Bengals of the NFL. The other for baseball would be built on land adjacent to the existing site of Riverfront Stadium (now called Cinergy Field). In 1996 Cinergy, a local energy company, bought the naming rights to Riverfront Stadium.

Players, Chicago White Sox

Eddie Cicotte — He was cruising along with a 21-10 record and 3.26 ERA then suspended three days before the end of the 1920 season, when the scandal of his receiving money from gamblers in the 1919 World Series broke in the press. Acquitted in the conspiracy trial on August 2, 1921, and forever banned from playing major league baseball by Commissioner Judge Kenesaw Mountain Landis, Eddie left a 14-year major-league career behind in which he was one of baseball's best pitchers.

His lifetime record was 208-149 with an ERA of 2.37. He was a practitioner of the infamous "shine ball," although he was skilled at throwing a knuckle ball as well. The "shine ball" thrown by Cicotte was a pitch that broke sharply as it approached the plate. The mechanics of the "shine ball" were that before delivering the ball, Cicotte rubbed his fingers on transparent paraffin coating on his uniform pant leg.

Following his banishment from baseball Cicotte felt a need to protect his family and took an assumed name. He went back to his hometown of Detroit and worked many years at the Ford Motor Company. He died on May 5, 1969, in Detroit.

Eddie "Cocky" Collins — Absolutely one of the all-time greats in baseball. Eddie had played from 1906–1914 for Connie Mack's Philadelphia

Athletics (including four World Series and winning three World Championships) before coming to Chicago in the 1915 season in exchange for $50,000 cash. In 1906 Collins had played under the name of Eddie Sullivan to conceal the fact that he was also a junior quarterback at Columbia University. After his identity became known he was permitted to finish his degree and then rejoined the Athletics.

After eight of his teammates were banished from baseball for alleged involvement in a conspiracy during the 1919 World Series, Collins became the White Sox's biggest drawing player. For seven consecutive seasons following the 1919 World Series Eddie would hit over .300 (1920–.369, 1921–.337, 1922–.324, 1923–.360, 1924–.349, 1925–.346, 1926–.344). He also led the American League in stolen bases in 1923 and 1924. During this same period the dismal White Sox would finish 2nd, 7th, 5th, 7th, 8th, 5th, 5th in the American League. In 1925 and 1926 he was the player-manager of the White Sox.

Then in 1927 he rejoined the Athletics and played four seasons primarily as a pinch hitter until 1930.

For 25 years service in the American League Eddie had a lifetime batting average of .333 with 3,311 hits and 743 stolen bases (fourth all-time behind Ricky Henderson, Lou Brock and Ty Cobb). Collins is also one of seven players who had more than 3,000 hits and that never won a batting title (Collins, Lou Brock, Paul Molitor, Dave Winfield, Eddie Murray, Robin Yount and Cal Ripken, Jr.).

He was elected to the Hall of Fame in 1939. After his playing days had ended he served in the Boston Red Sox front office from 1932 until his death on March 25, 1951, in Boston.

John "Shano" Collins— In 1920 Shano moved from the outfield to take over first base vacated by Chick Gandil who did not report to the White Sox spring training camp following the 1919 World Series. Subsequently, Shano hit .303 (his best season average ever) with 150 hits in 1920.

Then prior to the 1921 season on March 4, Shano along with Nemo Leibold was traded to the Boston Red Sox for veteran outfielder Harry Hooper (who had played in four World Series with the Red Sox and also had introduced sunglasses in the field). He continued to play for Boston through the 1925 season.

For 16 years in the major leagues Shano batted .264 with 1,687 hits. He eventually became manager of the Red Sox in 1931 finishing sixth, and then after finishing last in 1932 he was fired. He died on September 10, 1955, in Newton, Massachusetts.

Urban "Red" Faber— Arguably the White Sox's best pitcher overall, Faber had an 11-9 mediocre season record in 1919. He missed the World

Series due to illness but came back in 1920 to lead the White Sox pitchers with a 23-13 record, being one of four Chicago hurlers to win 20 games that season (Cicotte 21-10, Williams 22-14, Kerr 21-9).

Red, a spitball pitcher, was one of 18 pitchers allowed to continue to throw the wet one by special dispensation of the commissioner's office after it was banned from baseball in 1920.

With the banishment from baseball of Cicotte and Williams by baseball commissioner Judge Landis in 1921, Red became the bulwark of the White Sox staff. In 1922 he had a 25-15 record for a White Sox team that finished fifth in the American League. Then in 1923 for the third straight year he won 20 games (21-17), this time for the team that finished seventh in the league. He retired from baseball following the 1933 season.

Red had played for 20 years in the major leagues all for the Chicago White Sox. His career record was 254-213 with a 3.15 ERA. For a time after retirement as an active player he was the White Sox pitching coach, then he operated a bowling alley in Chicago for many years. In 1964 Red was elected to the Baseball Hall of Fame. He died at the age of 88 on September 25, 1976, in Chicago.

Oscar "Happy" Felsch—In 1920 Happy had a great season, hitting .338 with 188 hits and 14 home runs. But when the news broke of the alleged 1919 World Series scandal and he was indicted by the grand jury it was all over for him.

There were alleged reports after the fact that Happy had even continued to be involved with throwing ball games during the 1920 season. The jury hearing the conspiracy trial in the summer of 1921 acquitted him along with the other seven defendants. Nonetheless, he was banned from playing baseball again by Commissioner Judge Kenesaw Mountain Landis. Later Felsch would state publicly that he received $5,000 during the 1919 World Series.

Felsch had only been in the big leagues for six years but had already established himself as a superior center fielder that could not only hit well, but throw well too. He ended his career with a .293 lifetime batting average and 825 hits. However, in just six years he already had made 41 double plays in center field. By comparison his Hall of Fame contemporary Edd Roush made 49 double plays in 18 years. Later another Hall of Fame center fielder Duke Snider, played 18 years and only made 18 double plays.

After his banishment from the major leagues, Happy continued to play ball around his hometown of Milwaukee on sandlot teams and also worked as a crane operator and later ran a tavern. Also, along with two other alleged World Series conspirators, Swede Risberg and Joe Jackson, he sued the Chicago White Sox for back pay. On February 9, 1925, Happy was awarded $1,166, his back pay plus interest. He died on August 17, 1964, in a Milwaukee hospital as a result of a liver ailment.

Charles "Chick" Gandil— Chick did not report to spring training for the 1920 season. Later allegations have it that Gandil had received as much $35,000 for his participation in a conspiracy to throw the 1919 World Series.

Following his acquittal in the jury trial along with the seven other alleged White Sox conspirators and his lifetime banishment from baseball by new commissioner Judge Kenesaw Mountain Landis, he went out to the West Coast to live and became a plumber.

Chick had played in the major leagues for nine years and had a lifetime batting average of .277 with 1,176 hits. Also he had a lifetime fielding average of .992. He died on December 13, 1970.

Joe "Shoeless Joe" Jackson— Joe had a fine season in 1920 hitting .382 with 218 hits, while leading the American League in triples with 20. Then came late September and his suspension from baseball. At his grand jury appearance on September 28, 1920, Jackson admitted receiving $5,000 from his roommate Lefty Williams during the 1919 World Series. Of course on August 2, 1921, Jackson, along with the other seven alleged White Sox conspirators, was found not guilty in a jury trail. However, following the trial all eight players including Jackson were banned from ever playing major league baseball again by Commissioner Judge Kenesaw Mountain Landis.

Shoeless Joe Jackson had a brilliant 13-year major-league career in which he played 1,330 games and got 1,774 hits. His .356 career batting average is the third highest in major-league history. Jackson also holds the distinction of being one of two players in modern major-league history to have hit .400 in a season and not win a batting championship that year. In 1911, Joe Jackson's rookie season, he hit .408 but lost the batting crown that year to the Detroit Tigers' Ty Cobb who hit .420.

Joe was also a functional illiterate.

Although he admitted accepting money in the 1919 World Series, Jackson had always maintained his innocence on the field. He always held that he gave it everything he had in the 1919 World Series and his .375 batting average lends credence to that effect. In 1924 Joe sued White Sox owner Charles Comiskey for back pay on a three-year contract that he had signed in February 1920. Subsequently, a jury held that Jackson had not conspired to throw the 1919 World Series and was therefore entitled to the money owed him on his contract. Jackson was awarded $16,700. However, the judge in the trial found that Jackson had committed perjury in his testimony, as it was in conflict with his prior admission of guilt, overturned the jury's verdict and ordered him jailed. Later Jackson and Comiskey settled out of court.

Following his banishment from the major leagues, Joe continued to play ball in semi-pro leagues, ran a dry cleaning business and a liquor store, and at one point even went broke.

Over the years many individuals and groups attempted to have Jackson reinstated in baseball and therefore eligible for the Hall of Fame. Even in 1999, Ted Williams, Bob Feller and Hank Aaron were making attempts for reinstatement. However, all these attempts have been denied by a succession of commissioners from Judge Landis to Bud Selig.

The fans seemed to have forgotten Shoeless Joe Jackson too. In 1999 fans and baseball experts voted for the 30 player All-Century Dream Team. Twenty-five players were selected by the fans and a panel of baseball executives and experts selected five players. Eleven outfielders were named on the 30-player team, but Joe "Shoeless Joe" Jackson was not among them. Nonetheless, Bernard Malamud used Joe Jackson for the model of his character Roy Hobbs in "The Natural." Jackson died on December 5, 1951, in Greenville, South Carolina.

Bill "Big Bill" James— Following the 1919 World Series, Bill's eight-year big-league career came to an end. Prior to coming to the White Sox in August 1919 from the Boston Red Sox in exchange for cash, he had seen service with the Cleveland Indians, St. Louis Browns, Detroit Tigers and the Red Sox. His career won-lost record was 65-71 with an ERA of 3.20. He died on May 24, 1942, in Venice, California.

Richard "Dickie" Kerr— In 1920 Kerr won 21 games and lost 9 for the White Sox. The following year in 1921 he was 19-17 while pitching 308.2 innings for a seventh place club. Then following the season Kerr asked White Sox owner Charles Comiskey for a $500 raise. When pinch-penny Comiskey refused, Kerr left major league baseball behind and went home to Texas. He then became a holdout and although he was not supposed to play for any other organized team, he joined an independent team and ultimately wound up playing against a team that had a couple of the former White Sox players from the 1919 team on it who had been banned from baseball. Consequently, Kerr was suspended for a year. In 1925 Dickie did make a brief reappearance with the White Sox, pitching in just 12 games with a record of 0-1. Kerr then retired as a player.

His lifetime record for four major-league seasons was 53-34 with an ERA of 3.84.

He then began to manage various minor-league teams. It was while pursuing these endeavors that he converted a young pitcher by the name of Stan Musial into an outfielder, who went on to have a Hall of Fame career with the St. Louis Cardinals. Musial was so grateful to Kerr that he named his first son "Richard" after him. He died on May 4, 1963, in Houston.

Harry "Nemo" Leibold— In 1920 he played 108 games in right field for the White Sox. However, his batting average dipped 82 points from the previous season to .220.

On March 4, 1921, he was traded with Shano Collins to the Boston Red Sox for veteran outfielder Harry Hooper. In 1921 at Boston, Nemo's batting eye returned and he hit .306 with 143 hits in 123 games. He continued to play for the Red Sox until early in the 1923 season when he was sold May 26 on waivers to the Washington Senators. Once again he had a decent season hitting .305 while playing in 95 games for the Senators. Nemo finished his 13-year big-league career in style playing on consecutive American League pennant winners in 1924 and 1925 as a teammate of Walter "Big Train" Johnson. Johnson, 38 years old in 1925, was leading the Senators mound corps with back to back 20-game-win seasons. In the 1924 World Series in which the Senators defeated the New York Giants 4-3, Leibold hit only .167 in three trips to the plate. However, in the 1925 World Series that saw the Pittsburgh Pirates defeat the Senators 4-3, he made two plate appearances as a pinch hitter and had one hit, a double (.500). Nemo died on February 4, 1977, in Detroit, just a few days before what would have been his 85th birthday.

Grover Lowdermilk— A journeyman relief pitcher, he returned briefly to pitch in three games for the White Sox in 1920 (0-0, 6.75 ERA), then retired. Grover had a nine-year major-league career with a record of 23-39 and 3.58 ERA. During his tenure in the big leagues (1909–1920) he had pitched for six teams, the St. Louis Cardinals, Chicago Cubs, Detroit Tigers, Cleveland Indians, St. Louis Browns and the Chicago White Sox. He died on March 31, 1968, in Ordin, Illinois.

Byrd Lynn— Lynn, a back-up catcher to Ray Schalk, played his entire five-year major-league career with the White Sox. Byrd's last season was 1920. He appeared in 16 games, hitting .320. His five-year totals for 116 games are a batting average of .231, with 50 hits and 15 RBIs. For 88 games behind the plate he had a career fielding average of .969. He died on February 5, 1940, in Napa, California.

Erskine Mayer— Erskine's eight-year major league career came to an end following the 1919 World Series. He had begun his career with the Philadelphia Phillies in 1912 and was a member of the Phillies' 1915 National League pennant winning team. In fact Erskine had started the second game of the series against the Red Sox and went 9 innings losing 2-1. In July 1918 he was traded by the Phillies to the Pirates. Then in August 1919 with the White Sox about to enter the stretch drive against the Indians, Erskine was purchased by the White Sox on waivers. His lifetime won-lost record was 91-70 with an ERA of 2.96. He died on March 10, 1957, in Los Angeles.

Fred McMullin— As a utility infielder, he played in 46 games for the White Sox in 1920, hitting .197. Following his suspension at the end of the 1919 season and the acquittal of his seven indicted teammates in the 1921 conspiracy trial, McMullin was one of the eight players banned for life from playing major league baseball by Commissioner Landis. For six years in the big leagues, Fred had a lifetime batting average of .256, for 914 at bats in 304 games. He died on November 21, 1952, in Los Angeles.

Eddie Murphy— Murphy returned to play for the White Sox in 1920 and 1921 primarily as a pinch-hitter. In fact during the 1920 season he hit for an average of .339 with 40 hits in 118 at bats. After appearing in six games for the White Sox in 1921, Eddie was no longer on a major-league roster. However, in 1926 he reappeared briefly in the major leagues as a member of the Pittsburgh Pirates, appearing in 16 games for the most part as a pinch-hitter, batting .118. Eddie's 11-season big-league lifetime batting average was .287 with 680 hits while playing in 760 games. He also played in three World Series, 1912 and 1914 with the Philadelphia Athletics and 1919 with the White Sox. He died on February 21, 1969, in Dunmore, Pennsylvania.

Charles "Swede" Risberg— In 1920 Swede was hitting .266 and having another dismal year with the glove (fielding average of .934 with 45 errors) when he was one of the eight White Sox suspended with just three games to go in the season following the grand jury probe. Swede was a tough guy and rumors still persist that he threatened to kill Joe Jackson if he alerted White Sox officials that several players were accepting money from gamblers in the 1919 World Series.

While waiting for the trial to begin in 1921, Risberg, along with some of the other suspended White Sox players, Joe Jackson, Happy Felsch, Lefty Williams and Fred McMullin, attempted to start a barnstorming tour of Indiana and Wisconsin, but the tour fell apart when most of the local semi-pro teams scheduled to play them withdrew due to the controversy of the impending trial in Chicago.

Of course Risberg and all the other alleged conspirators were acquitted in August 1921, then suspended for life from playing major league baseball by Commissioner Judge Kenesaw Mountain Landis. Risberg had only been in the major leagues for four years, all with Chicago. He played in 476 games and had a lifetime batting average of .243 and a fielding average of .934 with 161 errors in 1.203 attempts.

Swede eventually settled in Minnesota and became a dairy farmer. Later he went back to his native northern California and operated a tavern. Those who knew Risberg said that he remained hard and defiant to the bitter end about the events of 1919. When he died on his 81st birthday, October 13, 1975, in Red Bluff, California, he was the last survivor of the eight suspended White Sox players.

Ray "Cracker" Schalk— Following the 1919 World Series, Ray continued to be the primary backstop for the White Sox until 1926 when be began sharing the duties with Buck Crouse.

In 1927 Ray replaced Eddie Collins as manager of the White Sox while remaining on the roster as a player. The following season on the morning of July 4, 1928, Ray resigned as manager effective the following day. However, before his resignation took effect he participated in a history-making event. Schalk had come up to the majors with the White Sox in 1912 and caught "Big Ed" Walsh (Hall of Fame 1946) when he was a member of the Sox (1904–1916). In 1928 Ed Walsh, the son of "Big Ed," was now a rookie pitcher on the White Sox. So on the morning of July 4, 1928, Schalk's last act as manager was to pencil himself in the lineup as catcher against the St. Louis Browns and thereby became the only major league catcher to ever catch a father-son combination in his career. This was the only game Schalk caught that season and the Sox lost that game to the Browns 11-8, with young Walsh going four innings. Just for the record, in 1908 Ed Walsh the elder had a season record of 40-15 for the White Sox.

In 1929 Ray Schalk appeared in five games for the New York Giants before retiring as a player.

In 18 years of big-league service Schalk played in 1,760 games and had a lifetime batting average of .253 with 1,345 hits. He was a much better than average defensive catcher too and retired with a lifetime fielding average of .981.

Following retirement, Ray returned as a coach on the White Sox for two years and then managed in the minors for nearly a decade, primarily in Buffalo. Later in life he managed a bowling alley in Chicago. He rarely talked about the events of 1919 and denied that he ever assaulted Lefty Williams after game two of the World Series or threatened Swede Risberg. In 1955 Ray was elected to the Baseball Hall of Fame in Cooperstown, New York. He died on May 19, 1970, in Chicago.

George "Buck" Weaver— Buck was having a fine season in 1920, hitting .333 with 210 hits, before he was suspended with three games remaining in the season along with seven of his White Sox teammates suspected of participating in a conspiracy during the 1919 World Series.

When the trial began in June 1921 Buck requested that he be tried separately from the other seven alleged conspirators, but was denied. He had maintained that he did nothing wrong and had played to the very best of his ability in the World Series, hitting .324. The long held theory of Weaver's involvement is that he sat in on conspiracy conferences and did not report them to officials. Also there has never been an allegation that Weaver received any money from gamblers during the series. Acquitted along with the other White Sox defendants in the trial, Weaver was nonetheless banned for life from baseball by Commissioner Judge Kenesaw Mountain Landis. A petition was signed by Chicago Masonic Lodge members with between 14,000 and 20,000 signatures on Weaver's behalf, but Judge Landis looked the other way. Whether fellow Masonic Lodge member and teammate Eddie Collins' signature was on the petition is not known.

In nine years in the major leagues Buck played in 1,254 games and had a lifetime batting average of .272 with 1,310 hits. Buck continued to play semi-pro ball after his banishment and in 1927 was playing just a few miles away from Comiskey Park for a team in Hammond, Indiana. Over the ensuing decades following the trial and subsequent edict of Judge Landis Buck appealed many times to the commissioner and his successors Happy Chandler and Ford Frick for reinstatement. It never came. Buck died on January 31, 1956, in Chicago still maintaining his innocence of any participation in a conspiracy.

Roy Wilkinson— In the 1920 season he had a 7-9 record with a 4.03 ERA for the White Sox. However, pitching in relief, his record for the year was 5-0 with 3 saves. In the 1921 season Roy had a backward record of 4-20 with an ERA of 5.13. He was out of the major leagues shortly after the 1922 campaign began after appearing in just four games for the Sox. For five years in the majors Roy had a career record of 12-31 with an ERA of 4.66. He died on July 2, 1956, in Louisville, Kentucky.

Claude "Lefty" Williams— In the 1920 season Lefty's record was 22-14 with an ERA of 3.19 when he was suspended along with the other seven alleged White Sox conspirators with three games left to play in the season. Of course Williams and the other alleged White Sox conspirators were acquitted by a jury trial in August 1921 and then Commissioner Landis suspended all of the players for life from baseball. The lifetime suspension terminated Lefty's promising career in the major leagues after seven seasons with a record of 82-48 and an ERA of 3.13.

Following his lifetime ban from baseball Williams operated a pool hall in Chicago for a time, then moved to California and began a plant nursery business. He died on November 4, 1959, in Laguna Beach, California.

Manager, Chicago White Sox

William "Kid" Gleason— Under Gleason's leadership the White Sox finished second in 1920 with rumors flying wildly that some of his players had dumped the pennant to the Cleveland Indians. He continued to manage the White Sox, now decimated by the lifetime suspensions given to eight of his players through the 1923 season. Then Gleason never managed another big-league team again. Kid had played in the major leagues from 1888–1912. First as a pitcher (1888–1895) with a career record of 134-134 and an ERA of 3.79. Then as a second baseman (1895–1912) with a career batting average of .261 and 1,944 hits. In 1890, pitching for the Philadelphia Phillies, he had a record of 38-17. Then in 1897, playing second base for the New York Giants, he hit .319 with 172 hits. Kid died on January 2, 1933, in Philadelphia.

Owner, Chicago White Sox

Charles "Chommy" "The Old Roman" Comiskey— With rumors rampant that some of his players had conspired to throw the 1919 World Series, Chommy put up a $10,000 reward for anyone that could provide him with proof that a conspiracy by any of his players had actually occurred. He never paid out that reward money though. At the end of the 1920 season eight of his players were implicated, and in the summer of 1921 there was the trial with the subsequent acquittals. Comiskey blamed American League President Ban Johnson for the scandal for not properly following-up on rumors that had been circulating during the 1919 World Series.

Following the trial and banishment of eight of his players by Judge Landis, Comiskey continued to run the White Sox as he always had, very frugally. He continued to deny raises to players that had produced on the field and even at one point released future Hall of Fame member Harry Hooper after the 1925 season when Hooper refused to take a cut in salary.

When Chommy died on October 26, 1931, in Eagle River, Wisconsin, he was still bitter about the events of 1919, thinking he had been cheated out of a World Championship and angry at Ban Johnson (fired as American League President January 1927). In 1939 Comiskey was posthumously elected to the Baseball Hall of Fame.

Team, Chicago White Sox

Charles Comiskey dedicated his new ballpark at 35th Street and Shields Avenue on Chicago's south side by laying a green cornerstone on

St. Patrick's Day, March 17, 1910. The White Sox would win a World Championship against the New York Giants in 1917 at Comiskey Park. Comiskey Park also served as the Chicago Cubs' home field for the 1918 World Series versus the Boston Red Sox with Babe Ruth pitching.

Following the 1919 World Series there wasn't much for White Sox fans to shout about for decades to come. The team, decimated by Judge Landis' banishment of several of its star players, struggled in the American League standings season after season. In the 1920 season the White Sox were in the pennant race right down to the final week of the season when the news of the alleged conspiracy broke and then they finished second just two games behind the Cleveland Indians.

However, following the 1920 season they would not finish in the first division again until 1935 when they would finish in fifth place with a record of 74-78 under player-manager Jimmy Dykes. The following is a list of where the Sox finished in the AL pennant race between 1921 and 1934 (7th, 5th, 7th, 8th, 5th, 5th, 5th, 5th, 7th, 7th, 8th, 7th, 5th, 8th).

Charles Comiskey remained in control of the White Sox until his death on October 26, 1931, at his summer home in Eagle River, Wisconsin. Following Chommy's death, the Comiskey family retained 46 percent of the White Sox stock, with his son J. Louis Comiskey becoming president and running the family business. In 1939 Charlie Comiskey was elected to the Baseball Hall of Fame.

On July 6, 1933, the first major league All-Star Game was played at Comiskey Park. Upper grandstand tickets for the game cost $1.10. The game was the vision of *Chicago Tribune* sports editor Arch Ward who convinced the club owners that the game would be of significant interest to the fans. In the 1933 All-Star Game a script could not have been written that was better than the actual outcome. A two-run home run by Babe Ruth in the third inning gave the American League a 3-0 lead and would stand up to be the edge needed in a 4-2 victory over the National League.

Two months later Comiskey Park would host the first black All-Star Game (the East-West game).

A steady performer for the White Sox from 1923–1942 and 1946 was Hall of Fame pitcher Ted Lyons. Lyons never played on a pennant winning team during his 21 years as a White Sox player, but still had a lifetime record of 260-230 with an ERA of 3.67.

During the period from 1930 to 1950 the White Sox star player and team leader was shortstop Luke Appling. Appling carried this ragamuffin team year after year. In 1936 when the White Sox finished second just two games behind the Detroit Tigers in the American League pennant chase, Luke Appling won the American League batting title with a .388 average and 128 RBIs. Appling would win his second batting title in 1943 with a .328 average. He finished his 20-year career in 1950 with a .310 lifetime batting average, with 2,749 hits and 1,116 RBIs. In 1964 Luke Appling was elected to the Baseball Hall of Fame at Cooperstown, New York. Playing in an Old-Timers game held in Washington, D.C., in 1982, 73-year-old Appling would hit a home run into the left field stands.

Following the 1955 season, Frank Lane, who had made the White Sox competitive again, resigned as general manager. In 1956 Chuck Comiskey, grandson of Chommy, became general manager. In 1957 he replaced Marty Marion as manager with Al Lopez.

Then in March 1959 Bill Veeck, Jr., bought operating control of the White Sox. Veeck had previously owned the St. Louis Browns and the Cleveland Indians. Finally, after 40 years, in 1959 the White Sox under manager Al Lopez would once again win the American League pennant. In tribute to the south-side champions, Chicago Mayor Richard J. Daley had all the civil defense air raid sirens turned on in the neighborhoods around Comiskey Park, including his own south-side neighborhood of Bridgeport. The 1959 White Sox were not a power-hitting team. In fact they had the fewest home runs (97) of any team in the league that year, as well as the second lowest team batting average (.250).

The 1959 White Sox were known as the "Go Go Sox" in deference to the speed that the team demonstrated on the base paths with a league leading 113 stolen bases led by shortstop Luis Aparicio's league leading 56 swipes and center fielder Jim Landis with 20. In addition, adding strength to the Sox defense up the middle at second base was eventual Hall of Fame member Nellie Fox, who had a fine season hitting .306 and leading the AL in fielding for second baseman with a .988 average.

The 1959 White Sox also had superb pitching led by Early Wynn 22-10 and Bob Shaw 18-6. The White Sox won the 1959 AL championship by five games over the second place Cleveland Indians and by 15 games over the powerful New York Yankees who between 1949 and 1958 had won the American League pennant nine times. However, in the 1959 World Series the White Sox would lose to the Los Angeles Dodgers 4-2.

In 1962 the Comiskey family's involvement with the White Sox came to an end when Charles Comiskey II sold his interest in the ball club to Arthur C. Allyn. During this period of time Bill Veeck also sold his interest in the club.

With falling attendance at Comiskey Park, in 1968 and 1969 the White Sox played 20 home games at Milwaukee's County Stadium, which had been abandoned by the Braves when they moved to Atlanta after the 1965 season. Rumors of the White Sox being sold or moved to another city were constantly in the air. When the 1972 players' strike delayed the opening of the season by eight days, Sox owner Arthur Allyn defied the other owners by permitting White Sox players to work out at Comiskey Park.

In the 1970s the White Sox weren't winning pennants but were becoming masters at promotion. The 1972 club featured rubber armed lefty Wilbur Wood who started both games of a double-header and finished the season with a record of 24-17. In 1976 Bill Veeck once again bought the club and brought his whacko ways back to Chicago. The White Sox introduced a scoreboard that exploded with fireworks when a player hit a home run. In the first game of a double-header against the Kansas City Royals on August 8, 1976, the White Sox players wore shorts. However, in the second game they wore pants. Perhaps the most notorious of the White Sox promotions took place on July 12, 1979, when the Sox hosted Disco Demolition Night. Fifty-thousand fans, most having paid 98 cents to get in, packed Comiskey Park for a double-header with the Detroit Tigers. Between games disco records were burned in a promotion hosted by radio station WLUP-FM. However, during the first game won by the Tigers 4-1, many fans began slinging their phonograph records like Frisbees onto the field. Then during the record-burning ceremony approximately 5,000 fans ran on to the field and would not return to their seats despite a personal appeal from White Sox Owner Bill Veeck. At that point, Chief Umpire Dave Phillips decided that the crowd was out of control, the field was a mess and suspended the second game. Shortly thereafter American League President Lee MacPhail declared the second game forfeited to Detroit.

In January 1981 for a second time, Veeck sold the White Sox. This time to a group of businessmen headed by Jerry Reinsdorf and Eddie Einhorn. Veeck then went into a quiet retirement often dining or having a few cocktails at Miller's Pub in the Loop, where he was accessible and friendly with the restaurant's staff and patrons alike. Also, in the early 1980s, on any given day during the summer, you could find Bill Veeck, Jr., on the North Side, sitting shirtless with the bleacher bums at Wrigley Field.

In 1983 the White Sox won the American League Western Division title by 20 games with a record of 99-63. The White Sox also set an attendance record in 1983, topping the 2 million mark for the first time ever. Unlike the 1959 "Go Go Sox" this pennant winning White Sox team was loaded with power and it scored a league leading 800 runs, led by the slugging of Ron Kittle, Harold Baines, Carlton Fisk and Greg Luzinski. The team also possessed a solid pitching staff led by Lamar Hoyt, 24-10, Richard Dotson, 22-7, and Floyd Bannister, 16-10. In the 1983 playoffs the White Sox played the AL Eastern Division Champion Baltimore Orioles. The White Sox won the first game 2-1 behind the seven-hit pitching of Hoyt, but didn't make it to the World Series as they lost the next three and the series to the Orioles, 3-1.

During the 1980s the new White Sox owners Reinsdorf and Einhorn kept public policy pressure mounting on the voters and state legislators at the state capitol in Springfield, Illinois, to build the team a new ballpark that they felt necessary to keep the White Sox competitive. There were the usual threats by Reinsdorf and Einhorn to move the franchise to another city and Sox owners shopped the club around to various western suburban communities in Chicago with voter referendums for a new stadium, all of which lost at the polls. Finally in the late 1980s the State of Illinois caved in to the mounting pressure from Reinsdorf and Einhorn and allocated $200 million of taxpayer money to build a new ballpark for the White Sox adjacent to Comiskey Park on the south side of Chicago.

On September 30, 1990, with Sammy Sosa playing in right field for Chicago, the last game was played in Comiskey Park between the Seattle Mariners and the White Sox. When Harold Reynolds of the Mariners grounded out ending the game and giving the Sox a 2-1 victory, the house that Chommy built came to an end after 80 years. Comiskey Park (1910–1990) was the oldest ballpark in the major leagues when it was closed.

The following April 1991 the new Comiskey Park opened and in 1993 the White Sox behind the power hitting of Frank Thomas won the American League Western Division championship for the first time in ten years. However, the Sox were defeated in the AL Championship Series by the Toronto Blue Jays 4-2. The following season major league baseball was restructured into three divisions in each league. In August 1994 the White Sox were leading the American League Central Division when the remainder of the season was canceled due to the players' strike.

The Reds vs. White Sox

Following the 1919 World Series the Cincinnati Reds and the Chicago White Sox would not play each other again in a regular- or post-season game until the advent of inter-league play 78 years later when they would meet at Cinergy Field in Cincinnati on Friday evening, June 10, 1997.

The Reds' stadium operations had the Opening Day bunting hung for the game and extra security was arranged for moody White Sox outfielder Albert Belle.

Both the Reds and White Sox were currently in fourth place in their divisions and 31,682 tickets were sold for the game, about the same number as for one of the 1919 World Series games between the two clubs.

Prior to the game Reds owner Marge Schott had requested that Albert Belle have his picture taken with her, but Belle rejected the request.

The White Sox won the game 3-1 on a two-run home run by Albert Belle over the fence in right center field in the top of the sixth off of Reds pitcher Pete Schourek.

Source Notes

Chapter 1

1. Christy Mathewson, *The New York Times*, October 2, 1919.
2. From an interview with Edd Roush, printed in *The Cincinnati Post*, 1985.
3. Bill Koch, *The Cincinnati Post*, 1987.
4. "Nerves May Decide It," *The New York Times*, October 1, 1919.

Chapter 2

1. From the sporting editor of *The Philadelphia Inquirer*, October 1, 1919.
2. Joe Villa for *The Philadelphia Inquirer*, October 1, 1919.
3. Joe Villa for *The Philadelphia Inquirer*, October 1, 1919.
4. From a Special to *The New York Times*, October 2, 1919.
5. From the sporting editor of *The Philadelphia Inquirer*, October 2, 1919.
6. From the sporting editor of *The Philadelphia Inquirer*, October 2, 1919.
7. From the sporting editor of *The Philadelphia Inquirer*, October 2, 1919.
8. Christy Mathewson, *The New York Times*, October 2, 1919.

Chapter 3

1. "Reds Now 7 to 10 Betting Favorites," *The New York Times*, October 2, 1919.
2. *The New York Times*, October 3, 1919.

3. From the sporting editor of *The Philadelphia Inquirer*, October 3, 1919.
4. From the sporting editor of *The Philadelphia Inquirer*, October 3, 1919.

Chapter 4

1. Hugh S. Fullerton, *The Cincinnati Post*, October 4, 1919.
2. Ren Mulford in *The Cincinnati Post*, October 4, 1919.
3. Hugh S. Fullerton, *The Cincinnati Post*, October 4, 1919.
4. Hugh S. Fullerton, *The Cincinnati Post*, October 4, 1919.
5. Tom Swope, *The Cincinnati Post*, October 4, 1919.
6. Tom Swope, *The Cincinnati Post*, October 4, 1919.

Chapter 5

1. Tom Swope, *The Cincinnati Post*, October 4, 1919.
2. Heinie Groh, *The Cincinnati Post*, October 4, 1919.
3. *The Cincinnati Post*, October 6, 1919.
4. *The Cincinnati Post*, October 6, 1919.
5. Ross Tenney, *The Cincinnati Post*, October 6, 1919.

Chapter 6

1. Editorial, *The Philadelphia Inquirer*, October 5, 1919.
2. "A Family Tree: The Origin of Pitches," *The [Newark] Star-Ledger*, April 2, 2000.
3. Grantland Rice, *The Cincinnati Post*, October 1919.
4. Grantland Rice, *The Cincinnati Post*, October 1919.
5. Heinie Groh, *The Cincinnati Post*, October 1919.
6. R.L. Goldberg, *The Philadelphia Inquirer*, October 7, 1919.
7. Grantland Rice, *The Cincinnati Post*, October 1919.
8. Heinie Groh, *The Cincinnati Post*, October 1919.
9. Jim Nasium, *The Philadelphia Inquirer*, October 7, 1919.
10. From a cartoon, "Eller's Shine Ball Shimmy!" *The Cincinnati Post*, October 1919.
11. Heinie Groh, *The Cincinnati Post*, October 1919.
12. Heinie Groh, *The Cincinnati Post*, October 1919.

Chapter 7

1. Ren Mulford, Jr., *The Cincinnati Post*, October 8, 1919.
2. Heinie Groh, *The Cincinnati Post*, October 8, 1919.
3. Ren Mulford, Jr., *The Cincinnati Post*, October 8, 1919.
4. Tom Swope, *The Cincinnati Post*, October 9, 1919.
5. Heinie Groh, *The Cincinnati Post*, October 8, 1919.

Chapter 8

1. Jim Nasium, *The Philadelphia Inquirer*, October 9, 1919.
2. Advertisement in *The Cincinnati Post*, October 6, 1919.
3. Tom Swope, *The Cincinnati Post*, October 9, 1919.
4. From the sporting editor of *The Philadelphia Inquirer*, October 9, 1919.
5. Heinie Groh, *The Cincinnati Post*, October 9, 1919.

Chapter 9

1. From a Special to *The New York Times*, October 9, 1919.
2. From a Special to *The New York Times*, October 9, 1919.
3. From the sporting editor of *The Philadelphia Inquirer*, October 9, 1919.
4. Jim Nasium, *The Philadelphia Inquirer*, October 9, 1919.
5. *The New York Times*, October 9, 1919.
6. *The New York Times*, October 9, 1919.
7. Jim Nasium, *The Philadelphia Inquirer*, October 9, 1919.

Chapter 10

1. *The Cincinnati Post* (date unknown).
2. *The Cincinnati Post* (date unknown).

Chapter 11

1. "7 Sox Involved in 1919 Baseball Mess," *The Philadelphia Inquirer*, September 23, 1920.
2. *The Philadelphia Inquirer*, September 24, 1920.
3. "Jury Convinced Crooked Work Was Done by Players in League with Gamblers," *The Philadelphia Inquirer*, September 25, 1920.
4. Grand jury testimony of Rube Benton, published in *The Philadelphia Inquirer*, September 25, 1920.
5. Statement of Charles Comiskey, published in *The Philadelphia Inquirer*, September 25, 1920.
6. *The Philadelphia Inquirer*, September 25, 1920.
7. "Heydler Challenges Proof of Crookedness," *The Philadelphia Inquirer*, September 25, 1920.
8. "Man Who Fixed 1919 World's Series Is Known," *The Philadelphia Inquirer*, September 25, 1920.
9. "Herrmann Will Gladly Take Witness Stand," *The Philadelphia Inquirer*, September 28, 1920.
10. "Dunn Confident, Starts Work on Stand," *The Philadelphia Inquirer*, September 28, 1920.

11. *The Philadelphia Inquirer*, September 28, 1920.

12. *The Philadelphia Inquirer*, September 28, 1920.

13. *"Say It Ain't So, Joe!" Great Moments in Baseball* by George L. Flynn (New York: Gallery Books, 1987).

14. *The Philadelphia Inquirer*, September 28, 1920.

15. *The Philadelphia Inquirer*, September 28, 1920.

16. *"Say It Ain't So, Joe!" Great Moments in Baseball* by George L. Flynn (New York: Gallery Books, 1987).

17. *The Cincinnati Enquirer*, September 29, 1920.

18. *The Philadelphia Inquirer*, September 29, 1920.

19. Grand jury testimony of Eddie Cicotte, from articles published in *The Cincinnati Enquirer* and *The Philadelphia Inquirer*, September 29, 1920.

20. Grand jury testimony of Joe Jackson, from articles published in *The Cincinnati Enquirer* and *The Philadelphia Inquirer*, September 29, 1920.

21. Official notification by Charles A. Comiskey of suspensions of eight Chicago White Sox players, from an article published in *The Cincinnati Enquirer*, September 29, 1920.

22. *The Cincinnati Enquirer*, September 29, 1920.

23. *The Philadelphia Inquirer*, September 29, 1920.

24. Sworn statement of Claude "Lefty" Williams, from *The Philadelphia Inquirer*, September 20, 1920.

25. *The Philadelphia Inquirer*, September 30, 1920.

26. *The Philadelphia Inquirer*, September 30, 1920.

27. *The Philadelphia Inquirer*, September 30, 1920.

28. "The Faith of Fifty Million People," *Baseball: An Illustrated History* by Geoffrey C. Ward and Ken Burns (New York: Alfred A. Knopf, 1994).

29. *The Cincinnati Enquirer*, September 29, 1920.

30. *The Cincinnati Enquirer*, September 29, 1920.

31. *The Cincinnati Enquirer*, September 29, 1920.

32. *The Cincinnati Enquirer*, September 29, 1920.

33. *The Philadelphia Inquirer*, September 30, 1920.

34. *The Philadelphia Inquirer*, September 30, 1920.

Chapter 12

1. *The Philadelphia Inquirer*, September 30, 1920.

2. *The Great Baseball Players from McGraw to Mantle* by Bert Randolph Sugar (Mineola, New York: Dover, 1997).

Bibliography

Astor, Gerald. *The Baseball Hall of Fame 50th Anniversary Book.* New York: Prentice Hall, 1988.

Bass, Mike. *Marge Schott Unleashed.* Champaign, Illinois: Sagamore Publishing, 1993.

Famighetti, Robert, ed. *The World Almanac and Book of Facts 2000.* Mahwah, New Jersey: Primedia Reference, 1999.

Flynn, George L. *Great Moments in Baseball.* New York: Gallery Books, 1987.

Golenbock, Peter. *Bums: An Oral History of the Brooklyn Dodgers.* New York: G. P. Putnam's Sons, 1984.

Honig, Donald. *The National League: An Illustrated History.* New York: Crown, 1983.

Hoppel, Joe, and Carter, Craig, eds. *Baseball: A Doubleheader Collection of Facts, Feats & Firsts.* New York: Galahad Books, 1992.

Lewis, Dottie L., ed. *Baseball in Cincinnati: From Wooden Fences to Astroturf.* Cincinnati: The Cincinnati Historical Society, 1988.

Microsoft. *Complete Baseball: The Ultimate Multimedia Reference for Every Baseball Fan.* Microsoft Corporation, 1994.

Sugar, Bert Randolph. *The Great Baseball Players from McGraw to Mantle.* Mineola, New York: Dover, 1997.

The WPA Guide to Cincinnati 1788–1943. Cincinnati: The Cincinnati Historical Society, 1987. Reprint of *Cincinnati: A Guide to the Queen City and its Neighbors* (The City of Cincinnati, 1943).

Ward, Geoffrey C., and Ken Burns. *Baseball: An Illustrated History.* New York: Alfred A. Knopf, 1994.

Wolff, Rick, ed. *The Baseball Encyclopedia.* 8th edition. New York: Macmillan, 1990.

Index

181